Lecture Notes
in Economics and
Mathematical Systems

Managing Editors: M. Beckmann and W. Krelle

355

Marc Salomon

Deterministic Lotsizing Models
for Production Planning

Springer-Verlag
Berlin Heidelberg New York London Paris
Tokyo Hong Kong Barcelona Budapest

Author

Dr. Marc Salomon
Erasmus University
Rotterdam School of Management
P. O. Box 1738
NL-3000 DR Rotterdam, The Netherlands

AL

ISBN 3-540-53701-5 Springer-Verlag Berlin Heidelberg New York
ISBN 0-387-53701-5 Springer-Verlag New York Berlin Heidelberg

Printing and binding: Druckhaus Beltz, Hemsbach/Bergstr.
2142/3140-543210 – Printed on acid-free paper

Acknowledgements

During the four years that it took to finish the research for this Ph.D. thesis, many people have supported me. First, I would like to thank my supervisors Prof. Jo van Nunen and Prof. Luk Van Wassenhove. Jo was always good-humoured and it was very stimulating to work in his group at the Rotterdam School of Management. Luk -who moved during this research project from Leuven to Rotterdam and then from Rotterdam to Fontainebleau- inspired me to start working on lotsizing problems. His expertise and encouragements were of great importance for realizing this thesis.

Moreover, I am thankful to the committee members Prof. A.H.G. Rinnooy Kan and Prof. J. Wessels for carefully reading this manuscript.

Also, I am deeply indebted to my colleagues Roelof Kuik and Leo Kroon. Beside that Roelof and Leo gave me great support in doing this research, they were also very patient and sensitive discussion partners in the many discussions that we had concerning subjects other than research.

Furthermore, I am grateful to Stan van Hoesel of the Econometric Institute at the Erasmus University Rotterdam, and to Johan Maes and Dirk Cattrysse of the Division of Industrial Management at the Katholieke Universiteit Leuven (Belgium). I highly appreciated the way in which Stan, Johan, and Dirk worked with me.

Moreover, I would like to acknowledge Prof. Fleischmann of the Business Administration Department at the University of Hamburg (FRG), who introduced a number of interesting lotsizing problems to me.

I am also thankful to the people of the Rotterdam School of Management and the Econometric Institute, who made my stay at the Erasmus University a very pleasant one.

Last but not least, I am very grateful to my family, who encouraged and supported me in the best way they could.

March 1991
Marc Salomon

Contents

II Multilevel Lotsizing Problems

Chapter 1

Introduction

This thesis deals with *timing* and *sizing* decisions for production lots, and more precisely, with *mathematical models* to support *optimal* timing and sizing decisions. These models are called *lotsizing* models. They are characterized by the fact that production lots are determined based on a *trade-off* between *production costs* and *customer service*.

Production costs can be categorized as *basic production costs*, which consist of material costs, labour costs, machine startup costs and overhead costs, and *inventory related costs*, which include costs of capital tied up in inventory, insurances and taxes.

Customer service is the capability of the firm to deliver to their clients the products in the quantity they ordered at the agreed upon time and place. The costs of realizing a certain service level are usually very difficult to convert into money. They include costs of expediting, loss of customer goodwill, and loss of sales revenues resulting from the shortage situation.

To keep production costs low and to realize a high service level are both utmost important objectives for the continuity and growth of a firm. Nevertheless, when planning production in such a way that these objectives are achieved as well as possible, a firm has often to deal with a number of problems. First, the production process can be very complex, which is the case when complicated interdependences and precedence relations exist between end-products and components in the production network. In this sort of production networks, usually termed *multilevel product structures*, production of end-products can only start when components are sufficiently available. Typical for these situations are coordination problems between production facilities at different levels in the product structure. It is evident that such problems have to be suitably solved in order to ensure an efficient production process in which end-products are delivered on time.

Another complicating factor is the presence of *bottle-necks* in the production process, a situation which occurs when demand for production capacity temporarily exceeds available production capacity, or when buffering through inventories is not feasible. These bottle-necks hinder the flow of goods through the production network, which leads to delays in production and consequently to poor customer service. Therefore, accurate capacity planning is essential in bottle-neck situations.

Finally, an important economic problem is caused by the fact that production costs and service (costs) are in fact *opposing forces*. Low production costs are achieved *(i)* when the production rate is smooth and capacity is fully utilized, often resulting in inflexible production strategies, which do not permit for fast interventions in the production plan, and *(ii)* when the inventory positions are kept low. Nevertheless, such a production policy may lead to long delivery times, causing an undesirable poor service level. On the other hand, when the firm has the strategy to offer a high service level with an immediate delivery of orders, this results either in considerable basic production costs, due to high flexibility, or in high inventory costs, due to large (safety) stock positions.

The earliest class of production planning models, explicitly dealing with the above-mentioned problems, is the famous *Economic Order Quantity* (EOQ) model, developed by F.W. Harris [57] in 1913. This model assumes a simple one-product, one-machine situation with instantaneous replenishments in which demand is stable and inventory holding costs and machine setup costs are *deterministic* and constant over time.

The solution to this model is widely known as *Wilson's lot-size formula*, since R.H. Wilson claimed to be the first to use this formula in practice. After introduction of the EOQ model, Wagner and Whitin [107] published on an extension of this model in 1958, in which time-phased dynamic demand over a finite planning horizon is considered.

In the late fifties Manne [84], and in the sixties and seventies Lasdon and Terjung [74], Zangwill [112], and Veinott [104], among others started working on lotsizing models for more complex manufacturing situations, in which multiple products, capacity restrictions, machine setup times and multilevel product structures play an important role. This line of research has continued to this date (1990), and has resulted in a large number of widely known model formulations and solution procedures for difficult production planning problems, like the *Capacitated Lotsizing Problem* (CLSP), the *Economic Lotsizing and Scheduling Problem* (ELSP), the *Multilevel Lotsizing Problem* (MLLP) and more recently, the *Discrete Lotsizing and Scheduling Problem* (DLSP).

Besides the more *theoretical* work on lotsizing models, a large number of researchers have worked on solving lotsizing problems in *practice*. The considerable number of publications in international specialist journals reporting on successful lotsizing applications in industry, e.g. by Günther [54], Rhodes [91], Van Nunen and Wessels [87], Van Wassenhove and De Bodt [102] and Van Wassenhove and Vanderhenst [103], demonstrates that research on lotsizing models and solution procedures is not only of *theoretical interest*, but also of large *practical value*.

This chapter is further organized as follows. First, we place the role of lotsizing in a conceptual cadre, and demonstrate its relation to other production planning problems. To do so, we introduce in Section 1.1 a well-known classification for planning problems, based on Anthony's framework.
After that, we establish in Section 1.2 the significance of lotsizing in modern production planning systems, by introducing some well-known systems (MRP, JIT, OPT), and by explaining the way in which these systems support the planner in taking lotsizing decisions.
Finally, this chapter is concluded in Section 1.3 with the statement of research motivations and objectives as well as with a concise description of the contents of subsequent chapters (Section 1.4).

1.1   Anthony's framework for planning

Production can be viewed as a *transformation process* in which *raw materials* are transformed into *end products*. These transformations are, however, not possible without *production resources* and their *planning*. A well-known framework to *categorize* planning problems was defined by Anthony [5] in 1965. According to this framework, (production) planning problems are classified into three categories:

- *Strategic (long range) planning problems.*

- *Tactical (medium range) planning problems.*

- *Operational (short range) planning problems.*

Strategic Planning

Anthony defines strategic planning problems as *"the process of deciding on the objectives of the organization, on changes in these objectives, on the resources used to attain these objectives, and on the policies that are to govern the acquisition, use, and disposition of these recourses"*. These decisions are extremely important because, to a great extend, they are responsible for maintaining the competitive capabilities of the firm, determining its rate of growth, and eventually defining its success or failure. An essential characteristic of these strategic decisions is that they have longlasting effects, thus forcing long planning horizons and a high level of aggregation in their analysis. This, in turn, requires the consideration of uncertainties and risk attitudes in the decision making process. Long range planning decisions include (des)investment decisions, product-mix decisions, decisions with respect to facility location and decisions concerned with plant design.

Tactical Planning

Tactical planning is defined by Anthony as *"the process by which managers assure that resources are obtained and used effectively and efficiently in the accomplishment of the organization's objective"*. They usually involve the consideration of a medium range time horizon, divided into several periods, and require significant aggregation of the relevant managerial information. Typical medium range planning decisions are purchasing of raw materials, maintenance planning, planning of workforce, pricing, order acceptance strategy and lead time determination. Aggregate production and inventory planning (lotsizing) also belong to this category of planning problems.

factor	strategic planning	tactical planning	operational planning
purpose	management of change, resource acquisition	resource utilization	execution, evaluation, and control
implementation instruments	policies, objectives, capital investments	budgets	procedures, reports
planning horizon	long	medium	short
scope	broad, corporate level	medium, plant level	narrow, job shop level
level of management involvement	top	middle	low
frequency of re-planning	low	medium	high
source of information	largely external	external and internal	largely internal
level of aggregation of information	highly aggregated	moderately aggregated	detailed
required accuracy	low	medium	high
degree of uncertainty	high	medium	low
degree of risk	high	medium	low

Table 1.1. Anthony's framework for planning.
Source: Hax and Candea [58]

<u>Operational Planning</u>

Operational planning problems are defined by Anthony as: *"the process of assuring that specific tasks are carried out effectively and efficiently"*. Decisions taken at the operational planning level are concerned with production sequencing, acceptance policy for rush orders, coordination of workforce, coordination of maintenance and coordination of inventory. Although most of the lotsizing problems considered in this thesis primarily focus on medium range planning, some models deal with operational planning problems also.

Some of the major elements of Anthony's framework for production planning are summarized in Table 1.1.

1.2   Developments in production planning

The intention of this section is to give a brief overview of the most important developments in production planning *concepts* over the last twenty years, and to touch briefly on the relation of these concepts with lotsizing.
Consecutively, the concepts of *Hierarchical Production Planning, Material Requirements Planning, Just In Time Manufacturing, Optimized Production Technology* and the role of lotsizing within these concepts are addressed. More extensive overviews on comparisons between planning concepts and their relation to lotsizing are given by e.g. Gelders and Van Wassenhove (1981) [47] and Buxey (1989) [21].

<u>Hierarchical Production Planning</u>

The Hierarchical Production Planning (HPP) approach, advocated by Hax and Meal (1975) [59], and by Bertrand and Wijngaard (1986) [13], among others, suggests to partition the overall planning problem into subproblems. The subproblems are chosen such that if one *"goes down"* in this planning hierarchy, the planning horizon decreases while the level of detail increases. In this *top-down* approach, higher level decisions impose constraints on lower-level actions. Typically, three planning levels are distinguished:

1. *The aggregated planning level:* Given aggregated time-phased demand (forecasts) for end products, the production quantities (lot sizes), inventory levels and workforces are determined over a *medium* range planning horizon.

2. *The components (item) level:* Given time-phased production quantities for end products, lot sizes for components (items) are determined over a medium range planning horizon.

3. *The operational planning level:* Given the (disaggregated) requirements for components, detailed production schedules are determined for a short-range planning horizon.

Since the decisions taken at any level in the planning hierarchy are more or less isolated from decisions taken at other levels, inconsistencies are not excluded. However, since real-life production planning problems tend to be very complex, solution procedures that solve the entire planning problem in a single step are out of the question. The hierarchical production planning approach is therefore a valuable alternative for solving difficult production planning problems.

Material Requirements Planning.

In a complex manufacturing situation where end products are manufactured from a large number of subassemblies, each in turn consisting of a large number of components, proper coordination of materials-flow is required. Material Requirements Planning (MRP), introduced in the late fifties, (see e.g. Orlicky [88]) is a *bottom-up* approach often used to coordinate goods flows in multilevel production-inventory environments. The system supports two important types of decisions:

1. Computation of time-phased requirements for all items at each level in the product structure, based on time-phased demand (forecasts) for end products and manufacturing lead times.

2. Computation of time-phased production quantities (lot sizes) to meet these requirements.

Besides a number of advantages offered by the use of MRP systems, like the simplicity and clarity of the concept and the availability of good software packages, MRP logic has a number of shortcomings. The most important shortcomings of MRP are:

- Calculation of lotsizes is based on the rather unrealistic assumption of infinite production capacity,

- Cost aspects are mostly ignored when lotsizes are calculated,

- Operational planning decisions are not adequately supported,

- Detailed data must be collected and updated.

However, some of the above mentioned shortcomings of MRP are partly resolved in new system implementations. In a system extension, named MRP II, modules for e.g. shop floor control and cost calculation are available.

Just In Time Manufacturing

Just In Time (JIT) manufacturing is a production planning philosophy originally applied by some Japanese manufacturing firms in the sixties. The main differences between MRP and JIT systems are twofold:
First, MRP is a *push* system, where the allocation of inventory is decided *centrally* for the whole system, taking into account the requirements and stock availabilities in the production network, while JIT is a *pull* system since the allocation of inventory is controlled by the inventory status of the *individual* stocking points in the production network. This central (MRP) versus local (JIT) decision control leads to different requirements for the information systems. To run a MRP system, a large amount of detailed information is necessary and therefore a high performance (and expensive) computer system is needed. For JIT systems less (detailed) information needs to be stored, and often it suffices to use simple forms (sometimes called *Kanbans*) instead of expensive computer facilities to run the system. *Second*, JIT is a *rate* based production control system in which the production rate is *equal* to the demand rate. In the ideal situation, when demand can be

estimated perfectly, this of course leads to *stockless* production. Advantages of stockless production are evident: low space requirements, reduced (inventory) handling and control costs and low inventory investments. However, for a successful implementation of the system, JIT requires stable and high-volume demand, while machine setup costs and machine setup times must be negligible. Unfortunately, such a manufacturing environment cannot always be achieved, in which case one is compelled to use alternative systems, like push systems or mixtures of push and pull systems.

Optimized Production Technology.

Optimized Production Technology (OPT) is a software package for production planning developed in the seventies. It consists of the following planning modules:

- *Buildnet:* This part of the system creates the production network and describes interactions between orders, products, raw materials and production resources.

- *Serve:* Based on time-phased demand (forecasts), lotsizes for components are computed in a similar way as for MRP, thereby disregarding capacity restrictions on workcenters. Output of this module is a time-phased capacity load profile which is used to identify bottle-necks in the production network.

- *Split:* Based on the capacity load profile computed by Serve, this module divides the production network into a *critical* part, which includes all bottle-neck workcenters, and a *noncritical* part.

Production quantities for products produced on noncritical workcenters are computed by Serve, while production on bottle-neck machines is planned by a fourth module called *Brain of OPT*. Although the logic of Brain of OPT is kept secret by its designer, Dr Goldratt, it is suspected that the module consists of a computer simulation and mathematical (optimization) techniques which solve (capacitated) lotsizing problems.

In contrast to MRP systems, OPT supports operational planning and is one of the few production planning concepts which takes capacity limitations explicitly into account when computing production lots.

Lotsizing.

Summarizing, lotsizing problems occur in the above-mentioned planning systems at the following levels in the planning hierarchy:

- In Hierarchical Production Planning systems, lotsizing decisions are taken at the aggregate and at the components (item) planning level. In most studies concerned with the system, simple linear programming models or more complex (mixed) integer programming models are suggested to determine workforces, lotsizes and inventory levels simultaneously.

- In Material Requirements Planning lotsizing decisions form an essential part of the logic. However, most of the MRP implementations use no complex mathematical models or decision rules, but instead use simple level-by-level heuristics to determine lot sizes in the complex multilevel production inventory situation. As Maes [79] investigated, only very few of the implemented lotsizing heuristics take capacity restrictions explicitly into account.

- In Just In Time (JIT) manufacturing hardly any complex lotsizing models are needed because of the assumptions of stability in demand and simplicity of the manufacturing process. Here, the problem of determining output rates is shifted to the design and control of the manufacturing process (line balancing).

- In Optimized Production Technology (OPT) the exact role of mathematical lotsizing models is unknown. However, it is suspected that in the module Serve an uncapacitated lotsizing problem is solved (in the same way as MRP does, by exploding demand), while in Brain Of OPT a capacitated lotsizing problem is solved in some way (using mathematical optimization techniques or trial and error procedures).

Table 1.2 summarizes the relationship between the aforementioned production planning systems and lotsizing.

Table 1.2. Lotsizing in modern production planning systems.			
name of the system	functionality	production control	lotsizing
HPP	short, medium and long range planning	centralized	(mixed-integer) linear programming approaches
MRP	medium range planning	centralized (push system)	simple heuristics, not dealing with capacity limitations
JIT	short range planning	decentralized (pull system)	not supported
OPT	short and medium range planning	centralized	simulation and/or heuristics dealing with capacity limitations

1.3   Research motivations and objectives.

The previous discussion has argued that lotsizing problems play an important role in modern production planning systems, like HPP, MRP, JIT and OPT. Therefore, research to develop and improve solution procedures for lotsizing problems is of eminent importance. Although many interesting real-life problems remain unsolved, a still growing number of them can be solved successfully, thanks to considerable research efforts.

For relatively simple manufacturing environments, dealing with one product and production capacity sufficiently available, efficient solution procedures have been found. Well-known and already mentioned results of these efforts are e.g. the EOQ-formula and the Wagner-Whitin algorithm. Nonetheless, when the manufacturing process is more complicated, as will often be the case in practice, problem complexity may increase formidably. Complicating factors in the manufacturing process are e.g.

- Dynamic demand,

- Nonlinear cost structures,

- Multilevel product structures,

- Capacity restrictions,

- Setup times,

- Sequencing and scheduling aspects

Notwithstanding a number of different models and solution procedures have been proposed which deal explicitly with such real-life situations, many of them can still not be solved satisfactorily.

The *objective* of the research reported on in this thesis is to make a contribution to the solution of some difficult lotsizing problems in which the above mentioned factors are present. The study contains several elements:

- *Literature study:*

    The literature dealing with deterministic lotsizing problems and solution procedures has been studied extensively. Based on this literature overview, new directions for attacking several lotsizing problems, like e.g. alternative model formulations and/or solution procedures, have been developed.

- *Analysis of problem complexity:*

    For a number of specific problems the mathematical complexity of the corresponding model formulation is determined. This is not only of theoretical interest, but also gives valuable information with respect to required computation times when solving larger sized problem instances.

- *Design of solution procedures:*

  A selection of some generally applicable solution procedures, like e.g. *dynamic programming, mathematical programming, polyhedral combinatorics, (Lagrangean) relaxation, Dantzig-Wolfe decomposition* and *statistical search* have been applied to solve several problem formulations.

- *Testing of solution procedures:*

  To obtain insight in the robustness of the proposed solution procedures in terms of quality of the solutions and required computation times, each procedure is tested on a large number of (randomly generated) data sets.

Although we feel that a study on the practical *implementation* of lotsizing procedures (e.g. embedding of lotsizing procedures in HPP or MRP systems), and on *organizational implications* can be very useful, such a study will be very time consuming and deserves therefore to be the subject of a research project in itself. For this reason we will refrain from studying these aspects in this thesis.

1.4   A guided tour through the thesis

This thesis consists of two parts. *Part I* deals with single level lotsizing models and solution procedures, whereas *Part II* is concerned with multilevel lotsizing models and solution procedures.

Contents of part I.

Chapter 2 introduces the single level lotsizing problem (Section 2.1). After a general discussion, we establish in Section 2.2 a *framework* due to Hackman and Leachman [55], for mathematical formulations of production planning problems. This framework defines a *metamodel* for lotsizing, from which a large class of well-known lotsizing models can be derived explicitly (Section 2.3). In Section 2.4 we present a literature overview of model formulations and solution procedures for *uncapacitated* lotsizing problems, like the *Economic Order Quantity Model*

(EOQ) and the *Wagner Whitin Model* (WW). In Section 2.5 we consider model formulations and algorithms for a number of well-known *capacitated* lotsizing problems, like the *Economic Lotsizing and Scheduling Problem* (ELSP), the *Capacitated Lotsizing Problem* (CLSP), the *Continuous Setup Lotsizing Problem* (CSLP), and the *Discrete Lotsizing and Scheduling Problem* (DLSP).
Finally, we summarize our discussion on single level lotsizing problems in Section 2.6.

In *Chapter 3* some extensions of the *Discrete Lotsizing and Scheduling Problem* (DLSP) are discussed (Section 3.1). These extensions include problems with parallel machines, problems with *sequence-dependent* setup costs and problems with *setup times.*
In Section 3.2 a standard problem notation is suggested, and for all problems covered by this notation *computational complexity results* are derived in Section 3.3. The chapter is concluded with a summary and a discussion of the results (Section 3.4).

A discussion of solution techniques for *single item* DLSP problems is given in *Chapter 4*. After an introduction of the problem in Section 4.1, the problem is formulated as an integer program (IP) in Section 4.2. In addition, a set of *valid inequalities* is derived which can be added to the LP-relaxation of the integer program, to obtain stronger lower bounds in e.g. branch-and-bound procedures to solve IP. Section 4.2. is ended with an explanation of a straightforward *dynamic programming* algorithm for problems with general cost structures. In Section 4.3 we present an *alternative formulation* for the single item DLSP, based on an IP formulation for the *assignment problem.* For this formulation we show that under special restrictions with respect to the input parameters its LP relaxation yields all-integer solutions.
Finally, for problems with special cost structures a *fast* dynamic programming algorithm is introduced in Section 4.4. A summary and a discussion of the results (Section 4.5) ends this chapter.

Chapter 5 deals with *multi-item* DLSP problems. After a general introduction to the problem (Section 5.1), polynomial time bounded DP algorithms are presented in Section 5.2 for problems with a fixed number of items and machines.

Fleischmann's algorithms for problems with sequence independent and sequence dependent setup costs and zero setup times are discussed in Section 5.3. Two new heuristics for problems with nonzero setup times are proposed in Section 5.4. These heuristics are based on *column generation techniques* (Dantzig-Wolfe decomposition) in combination with *dual ascent* and *subgradient optimization.*

In Section 5.5 a computational comparison is given between the heuristics on a set of test problems. Section 5.6 summarizes the results of Chapter 5.

Contents of Part II.

Chapter 6 presents an introduction to multilevel uncapacitated lotsizing models. In Section 6.1 a literature review is given and some well-known solution procedures are discussed for the *Multilevel Lotsizing Problem* (MLLP).

A new heuristic for MLLP is presented in Section 6.2, based on Lagrange relaxation, dynamic programming and subgradient optimization. Test results are presented in Section 6.3, and Section 6.4 summarizes the discussion in Chapter 6.

In *Chapter 7* a review is given of *capacitated* lotsizing models in a multilevel context, in particular the *Multilevel Capacitated Lotsizing Problem* (MLCLP). Three new heuristics for MLCLP are stated in Section 7.2, based on *simulated annealing, tabu search* and *linear programming* respectively. Finally, in Section 7.3 some computational results are given, and the chapter is concluded with a summary and a discussion of the results (Section 7.4).

The thesis ends with an Epilogue, which contains a concise overview of the thesis and points out some promising research directions.

Chapter 2

Model Survey

2.1 Introduction

This chapter reviews alternative model formulations for single level lot-sizing problems. In single level lotsizing problems the manufacturing process is described by a single level product structure, in which products are directly produced from raw materials without intermediate stocking points or subassemblies. Product demands are assessed from customer orders or market forecasts. This situation is often called *"in-dependent demand"*, since an item's requirements do not depend upon the lotsizing decisions for another item. Usually, single level lotsizing problems are classified into two categories. The first category consists of the *uncapacitated* problems, for which it is assumed that production resources are available in abundance, although the cost of setups is nontrivial. The ability to solve these problems has transfer value to more complex problems. The problem may also be sufficiently close to some real manufacturing environments, which have flexible resources (workforce and equipment) and considerable slack.

The second category corresponds to the *capacitated* problems, where availability of production resources is limited. The main problem here is caused by the fact that capacity requirements introduce an interdependency between items, which may lead to complex coordination problems. Additional difficulties are caused by significant machine setup times, sequencing aspects and dynamic demand. This problem is of interest for two reasons. First, it is found in several manufacturing settings. Plants with shallow bills of material, like breweries and paint producers, are good examples. Second, problems of this type may appear as sub-problems of more complex, multilevel problems.

Before giving an overview of uncapacitated lotsizing problems (Section 2.4) and capacitated lotsizing problems (Section 2.5), Section 2.2 discusses a *framework* for production planning based on *"A general framework for modeling production"* by Hackman and Leachman [55]. This framework defines a *metamodel* (Section 2.3), from which a large class of relevant lotsizing models, as discussed in the remainder of this chapter, can be derived. The chapter is concluded in Section 2.6, with a summary and a discussion.

2.2   A framework for production planning

In this section we consider a framework for production planning, due to Hackman and Leachman [55]. This framework is of interest for two reasons when studying lotsizing problems: First, it assesses accuracy and validity of the representation of a particular production process by a given model, and second, is can be useful when developing more accurate models, when existing models provide inadequate representations of the production process.

The framework models a production system as a *directed network* in which nodes represent *primitive production activities*, i.e. activities whose internal organisation is not modelled any further. Directed arcs indicate possible transfers of *intermediate products*. Intermediate products are outputs of one or more activities which serve as inputs to other activities. Production at each activity requires intermediate products transferred from other activities and/or *system exogenous inputs*. System exogenous inputs are of two types: *nonstorable services* and *storable materials*. Services include labour trades, machines and facilities, while materials include purchased parts, raw materials, fuels etc.

Each flow of a service or material is modelled as a bounded function of time, and there are two fundamental types of flows. The first and more common type, called a *rate based flow*, represents the rate -i.e. the quantity per unit time- of flow. The second type, called an *event-based flow*, represents the numerical value of an event at a certain point in time.

In each model, a joint *domain* reflects the domain of technologically feasible flows. The domain may involve complicated constraints linking different activities. For example, assume activities A and B represent production of products A and B, respectively. Suppose each activity uses the service of the same machine which can only process one type of product at a time. Then the flow domain should be defined to ensure that the machine does not produce for A and B simultaneous. Finally, for each activity a *dynamic production function* is formulated, which maps input flows applied at an activity into realized output flows.

Summarizing, a deterministic model of a specific production process is categorized by identifying and defining the abstract model elements: the activity network, the exogenous inputs, the intermediate and final products, the activity dynamic production functions and their domains.

2.3 A METAMODEL for lotsizing

To represent a large class of single level lotsizing problems, a number of simplifications can be made with respect to the general framework of Section 2.2. For instance, when considering single facility lotsizing problems, the production network consists of one production facility and one stocking point only, and the primitive production activities are limited to production of multiple items on this facility. The relevant flows in the network are demand, production, and inventory. Typical for single level models is that inputs of the production activity are raw materials, labour and production capacity, while sub-assemblies do not occur as input or output of any production activity. Technical restrictions, modelled by domains on flows, define available production and inventory capacities, as well as conditions on e.g. production sequences. Outputs consist of end-products only, and production functions are usually such that the output flow of a certain production activity is proportional to its input flow.

Applying the above mentioned simplifications to the general framework, and adding an appropriate objective function, yields a METAMODEL for lotsizing. Mathematically, METAMODEL can be formulated as follows:

METAMODEL:

$$\min \int_0^T \left(v[x_1, .., x_N](t) + h[I_1, .., I_N](t) + o[c_1, .., c_K](t) \right) dt \qquad (2.1)$$

subject to

$$I_i(t) = I_i(0) + X_i(t) - D_i(t) \qquad i = 1, .., N \qquad (2.2)$$

$$g_k[x_1, ..., x_N](t) \le c_k(t) \qquad\qquad k = 1, .., K \qquad (2.3)$$

where the following symbols are used:

N = number of items.

T = length of planning horizon.

K = number of production resources.

t = time index.

i = item index ($i \in \{1, .., N\}$).

k = resource index ($k \in \{1, .., K\}$).

$D_i(t)$ = cumulative demand for item i at time t.

$I_i(t)$ = inventory position for item i at time t.

$x_i(t)$ = production rate for item i at time t.

$X_i(t)$ = cumulative production for item i at time t.
($X_i(t) = \int_0^t x_i(\tau)d\tau$.)

$c_k(t)$ = available capacity for resource k at time t.

$g_k(.)(t)$ = *capacity allocation* function of resource k at time t.

$v(.)(t)$ = production related costs at time t.

$h(.)(t)$ = inventory and backlogging related costs at time t.

$o(.)(t)$ = capacity related costs at time t.

In the formulation of METAMODEL, time 0 is defined as a reference point after which flows are determined by planning calculations using the model. Flows that occur before time 0 are assumed to be predetermined as input of the model.

The objective (2.1) is to minimize the sum of production flow related costs $v(.)$, inventory flow related costs $h(.)$, and capacity allocation related cost $o(.)$. Furthermore, equations (2.2) are the so called "balance-equations", which define the inventory flows based on a balance between demand and production. Finally, constraints (2.3) state the technological requirements, that production may never exceed available capacity for any resource k.

From METAMODEL a large number of lotsizing models, known from literature, can be derived. These models differ in the way assumptions are made with respect to a number of major components of META-MODEL. Following [46], these major components include:

- *Planning horizon and time scale*: The planning horizon may be *finite* or *infinite* ($T = \infty$), and the time scale is either *continuous*, or partitioned into a number of *discrete*[1] time buckets (planning periods). In case of a discrete time scale, distinction is made between *small* time buckets, and *large* time buckets. The difference consists herein, that "small" time bucket models allow for at most one item to be produced per period, while setups can be carried across period boundaries, whereas "large" time buckets models permit multiple items to be produced per period, but setups are disallowed to be carried over, even if production of a given product occurs in successive periods.

- *Demand rate*: Deterministic demand rate $d(t)$ is either assumed to be *constant* over time (which is typical for policy determining models in continuous time), or *dynamic*, in which case time-dependent demand is specified per period.

- *Service policy*: Usually, two types of service policies are distinguished. The first type *disallows* shortages, while the second type *allows* shortages, thereby possibly accounting for shortage costs.

---

[1]In case of a discrete time scale, the integral in (2.1) is replaced by a sum.

Responses to shortages are either modelled in terms of *backlogging* possibilities, in which case orders can be delivered after their agreed upon delivery time, or in terms of *lost sales*. In lost sales models, orders that can not be delivered at or before the due date are not accepted by the client, and will be lost.

- *Cost functions*: The way in which various lotsizing models account for costs differs substantially. The cost function $v(.)$, associated with the production rate $x(.)$, usually consists of a *fixed cost* part, and/or a *variable cost* part. Fixed costs include (nonlinear) machine setup costs, which may be time and/or sequence dependent, whereas variable costs consist of (time dependent) production costs, typically proportional to the amount produced. The cost function $h(.)$, associated with the inventory-rate $I(.)$, accounts for inventory holding costs. In case that shortage situations are allowed, the function also models its associated costs. Finally, the capacity related cost function $o(.)$ represents the cost of using regular capacity and/or extra capacity. The costs for using extra capacity include for instance the costs due to subcontracting or overtime work.

- *Resource constraints*: Capacity restrictions on resources, as modelled by constraints (2.3), are either absent, in which case we have an *uncapacitated* model (Section 2.4), or they are present, in which case we have a *capacitated* model (Section 2.5). Capacitated models may consist of multiple capacity allocation functions $g_k(.)$, which take into account *production rates* and/or *setup times*. Production rates are modelled by dynamic functions, and setup times possibly depend on production sequences. Furthermore, the available capacity for resource k, modelled by $c_k(.)$, is either fixed, or expandable (e.g. when over-time work is allowed).

In the discussion of Section 2.6 we present an overview of the similarities and dissimilarities between various lotsizing models, with respect to the aforementioned components.

2.4 Uncapacitated problems

The main concern for this class of problems is in determining production lots for multiple items over an (in)finite planning horizon, such that setup costs, inventory holding costs, production costs, and backlogging costs are minimized, while known demand is satisfied. There is no interdependency between items, because of the absence of capacity constraints and parent-component relationships. Therefore, lotsizing decisions can be made for each item separately.

In this section we discuss model formulations and solution procedures for two important uncapacitated lotsizing models, i.e. the *EOQ-model* (Section 2.4.1) and the *Wagner-Whitin* model (Section 2.4.2).

2.4.1 The EOQ-model

As already mentioned in Chapter 1, the first lotsizing model, explicitly dealing with the aforementioned type of problem setting, is the well-known EOQ-model, developed by Harris (1913) [57]. The basic model formulation assumes a continuous and infinite time axis, a constant demand rate, an infinite production rate, no backlogging possibilities, as well as constant setup and inventory holding costs. Using elementary calculus, it can be shown that under these assumptions the optimal production quantity is given by $\sqrt{2SD/h}$, where S is the setup cost, D is the demand rate, and h is the inventory holding cost.

Relaxations of the basic model assumptions are discussed by Hax and Candea [58], and include models that allow for finite production rates, backlogging, and quantity discounts.

2.4.2 The Wagner-Whitin model

An extension of the EOQ-model was suggested in 1958 by Wagner and Whitin [107]. They assume in their model a finite and discrete time axis, and allow for time varying demand, backlogging, and a general cost structure.

Model formulation.

The Wagner-Whitin model (WW) is formulated mathematically as follows:

WW:

$$\min \sum_{t=1}^{T} (v_t(x_t) + h_t(I_t)) \tag{2.4}$$

subject to

$$I_{t-1} + x_t - d_t = I_t \qquad\qquad t = 1, .., T \qquad (2.5)$$

$$I_0 = I_T = 0 \tag{2.6}$$

$$x_t \geq 0 \qquad\qquad t = 1, .., T \qquad (2.7)$$

where T is the number of planning periods, d_t is the demand in period t, $v_t(x)$ is the cost of producing x units in period t, and $h_t(I)$ models the cost of having I units in inventory at the end of period t, whenever $I \geq 0$, *or* the cost of having a shortage of I units at the end of period t, whenever $I < 0$. Decision variables in the model are the production quantity in period t, denoted by x_t, and the inventory or backlogging position at the end of period t, denoted by I_t. Equations (2.5) are the balance equations, defining inventory or backlogging positions. Moreover, equations (2.6) state that starting and ending inventory are zero, while (2.7) assures that production quantities are non-negative.

Computational complexity and algorithms.

To solve the Wagner-Whitin model, a large number of procedures have been developed. These procedures can be subdivided into two categories: *(i)* procedures that give *optimal* solutions to the problem, and *(ii)* approximation procedures, also called *heuristics*.

The traditional optimal solution procedures, suggested by Manne [84], and by Wagner and Whitin [107], make the following assumptions with respect to inventory positions and cost structure:

(a) Inventory positions are non-negative ($I_t \geq 0$), and consequently backlogging is disallowed.

(b) The production cost $v_t(x) = S_t + p_t x$ whenever $x > 0$, and $v_t(0) = 0$. Furthermore, $h_t(I) = h_t I$ and p_t is independent of t. Here, non-negative constants S_t, p_t and h_t are setup cost, production cost per unit, and holding cost per unit in period t, respectively.

Wagner and Whitin provide a dynamic programming algorithm, based on the zero inventory property ($I_{t-1} x_t = 0$). This algorithm has a running time of $\mathcal{O}(T^2)$.

In subsequent papers, a number of the aforementioned assumptions with respect to inventory positions and cost structure were relaxed. For instance, Wagner [108] showed that his dynamic programming algorithm can also be used in special cases when production costs (p_t) are time-dependent. Zabel [110] and Eppen et al. [37] relaxed the non-negativity conditions on production and holding costs, and require only $S_t \geq 0$ for all t. Further relaxations with respect to the cost structure were made by Zangwill [111], who allowed $h_t(.)$ to be an arbitrary non-decreasing concave cost function, and by Veinott [105], who showed that the problem is still solvable by an $\mathcal{O}(T^2)$ dynamic programming algorithm in case of general concave cost functions $v_t(.)$ and $h_t(.)$. Relaxations with respect to the sign of inventory variables, thereby allowing for backlogging, were made by Zangwill [111,112], among others.

Recently, significant improvements have been made to bring down the theoretical running time of the dynamic-programming algorithms. These improvements are based on the discovery of special (cost) structure properties of the problem, and on an appropriate choice of data-structures. Such new results are reported in papers by Wagelmans et al. [106], and by Aggarwal and Park [4], among others.

Table 2.1 presents an overview of the computational complexity of optimal solution procedures for the Wagner-Whitin problem, under different assumptions with respect to backlogging and cost structure. This overview is based on the results reported in [4].

Table 2.1. Complexity results for the WW-problem		
cost structure	no backlogging	with backlogging
$v_t(0) = 0$; $v_t(x) = S_t + p_t x$ for $x > 0$ $h_t(I) = h^+ \max(0, I) + h^- \max(0, -I)$ $S_t, h^+, h^-, p_t \geq 0$	$\mathcal{O}(T)$ even if $h_t(I) = h_t I$ when $p_t + h_{t+1} \geq p_{t+1}$	$\mathcal{O}(T)$ p_t constant for all t
$v_t(0) = 0$; $v_t(x) = S_t + p_t x$ for $x > 0$ $h_t(I) = h_t^+ \max(0, I) + h_t^- \max(0, -I)$ $S_t, h_t^+, h_t^-, p_t \geq 0$	$\mathcal{O}(T \log T)$	$\mathcal{O}(T \log T)$
$v_t(.)$ and $h_t(.)$ concave	$\mathcal{O}(T^2)$	$\mathcal{O}(T^2)$
Here, h^+ (h^-) are inventory holding (backlogging) costs respectively.		

Besides the optimal solution procedures for the WW-problem, a large number of heuristic procedures is available. The most prominent among them are the *Silver-Meal* heuristic [97], the *Least Unit Cost* heuristic [51], the *Part Period Balancing* heuristic [27], and the EOQ based *Period Order Quantity* heuristic [12]. In general, these heuristics assume *constant* setup costs, inventory holding costs, and production costs, while backlogging is *not* allowed. The theoretical running time of the heuristics is $\mathcal{O}(T)$. A recent overview, in which the above-mentioned heuristics are compared in terms of computational speed, is given by Baker [9].

Extensions.

The standard WW-model has been extended in several ways. Some models allow for negative demands, limits on inventory positions, limits on how long goods can be backlogged or stored, periodic demand functions, and periodic cost functions. For a more detailed overview of these model extensions, the reader is referred to [4].

2.5 Capacitated problems

In general, lotsizing in the presence of capacity constraints can be viewed as one of the most difficult problems in production planning. The main reason for this is that capacity constraints introduce a strong interdependency between lotsizing decisions for different items. As a consequence, it will be no longer possible to consider each item in isolation. From a mathematical point of view the need for a simultaneous contemplation of multiple items leads to larger and more complex model formulations, which turn out to be significantly harder to solve than models for uncapacitated problems. Furthermore, in practice, additional complications are introduced by the existence of multiple capacitated resources, nonzero setup-times, non-linear cost structures (setup costs) and sequencing aspects. In this section we present an overview of some well-known lotsizing models, which explicitly deal with capacity restrictions. Two "classical" problem formulations, known as the *Economic Lotsizing and Scheduling Problem* (ELSP), and the *Capacitated Lotsizing Problem* (CLSP), are discussed in Section 2.5.1 and in Section 2.5.2, respectively. An alternative problem formulation, called the *Continuous Setup Lotsizing Problem* (CSLP), is considered in Section 2.5.3. Finally, in Section 2.5.4 the *Discrete Lotsizing and Scheduling Problem* (DLSP) is introduced. This problem, its complexity, and algorithms are subject of further discussion in Chapters 3, 4, and 5.

2.5.1 The Economic Lotsizing and Scheduling Problem (ELSP).

The Economic Lotsizing and Scheduling Problem (ELSP) is concerned with finding cyclical production schedules for multiple items on a single machine, such that *(i)* the sum of setup costs and inventory holding costs is minimized, *(ii)* demand is fulfilled without backlogging, and *(iii)* no two items are produced at the same time. The time axis is assumed to be continuous and infinite, while demand rate, production rate, setup costs, and inventory holding costs are assumed to be constant over time.

Model formulation.

Mathematically, ELSP is formulated in terms of the following constrained objective function:

ELSP:

$$\min_{(T_1,..,T_N)\in\mathcal{F}} \sum_{i=1}^{N} \left(\frac{S_i}{T_i} + \frac{h_i d_i (1 - d_i/r_i) T_i}{2} \right) \tag{2.8}$$

where N is the number of items to be scheduled. Furthermore, for each item i, constants S_i, h_i, d_i, and r_i are the setup costs, the inventory holding costs, the demand rate, and the production rate, respectively. Decision variables T_i denote the *"cycle time"* for item i, that is, the time between two successive production runs for the same item i. Finally, the set $\mathcal{F}$ is defined as the set of all N-tuples $(T_1,..,T_N)$, for which the corresponding production schedules are feasible, i.e. for which no two items are produced at the same time.

Computational complexity and algorithms.

The Economic Lotsizing and Scheduling Problem is known as a notably hard problem in production planning. Hsu [62] proved that the problem is NP-Hard. Notwithstanding the complexity of the problem, a large number of authors have worked on solution procedures for ELSP. Elmaghraby [36] differentiates in his excellent overview on ELSP between two categories of solution procedures: *(i)* analytical approaches that find an *optimal solution to a restricted version of the problem*, and *(ii)* heuristic procedures that search for *acceptable solutions to the original problem.*

Analytical approaches to solve ELSP include the *common cycle* approach, due to Hanssmann [56], and the *basic period* approach, due to Bomberger [19]. The common cycle approach assumes the set $\mathcal{F}$ to be restricted to N-tuples for which $T_1 = ... = T_N = T$, where T is the length of the common cycle. The basic period approach assumes the set $\mathcal{F}$ to be restricted to N-tuples for which $T_i = n_i T$, where n_i are

integer multipliers of the common cycle length T. For both approaches
it holds, that once a feasible common-cycle length T has been determined (iteratively, usually by some search method), the minimal cost
schedule and the corresponding multipliers n_i can be determined easily
(for the common cycle approach by simple calculus, and for the basic
period approach by a dynamic programming algorithm, which may be
rather time consuming). Extensions and adaptations of the common
cycle and the basic period approach are reported by Elmaghraby [36],
Axsäter [7], and Hendriks and Wessels [60], among others.

Heuristic approaches to solve ELSP are usually based on the basic period approach (although some exceptions exist, e.g. the heuristics by
Delporte and Thomas [28], and by Dobson [32]). The "basic period"
heuristics consist of three main components: *(i)* a procedure to compute the parameters n_i and T, and *(ii)* a procedure to detect whether
a given choice of parameters is infeasible, and *(iii)* a rule to modify
the multipliers in case of infeasibility. Although *(i)*, and *(iii)* are based
on straightforward calculations, the problem one is faced with at *(ii)*
is shown to be NP-Complete (see [62]). Therefore, the procedure that
deals with the feasibility problem is frequently of heuristic nature in
itself. Heuristics of the "basic period" type have been proposed by
Madigan [78], Stankard and Gupta [99], Doll and Whybark [34], and
Goyal [52], among others. A computational comparison between them
is found in [36].

Extensions.

Model extensions for ELSP address problems with nonzero setup times
(Fujita [43] and Dobson [32]), sequence dependent setup costs and times
(Dobson [31]), parallel machines (Carreno [22]), family setup costs, and
group discounts (see Silver and Peterson [98]).

2.5.2   The Capacitated Lotsizing Problem (CLSP)

The Capacitated Lotsizing Problem (CLSP) is the problem of determining a time-phased production schedule for multiple items on a single
machine, such that the sum of setup costs, inventory holding costs,

and production costs is minimized. Dynamic demand for each item is specified per period, and backlogging is not allowed. Moreover, in each period total production must be within bounds set by a capacity constraint.

Model formulation.

Mathematically, CLSP is formulated as follows:

CLSP:

$$\min \sum_{i=1}^{N} \sum_{t=1}^{T} (S_i y_{i,t} + h_i I_{i,t} + p_{i,t} x_{i,t}) \tag{2.9}$$

subject to

$$I_{i,t-1} + x_{i,t} - d_{i,t} = I_{i,t} \qquad\qquad i = 1,..,N;\ t = 1,..,T \quad (2.10)$$

$$\sum_{i=1}^{N} b_i x_{i,t} \leq C_t \qquad\qquad t = 1,..,T \tag{2.11}$$

$$x_{i,t} \leq \left(\sum_{\tau=t}^{T} d_{i,\tau} \right) y_{i,t} \qquad\qquad i = 1,..,N;\ t = 1,..,T \quad (2.12)$$

$$x_{i,t}, I_{i,t} \geq 0 \qquad\qquad i = 1,..,N;\ t = 1,..,T \quad (2.13)$$

$$y_{i,t} \in \{0,1\} \qquad\qquad i = 1,..,N;\ t = 1,..,T. \quad (2.14)$$

where N is the number of items, and T is the number of time periods. Moreover, S_i, h_i, $p_{i,t}$, b_i, and $d_{i,t}$ are setup costs, inventory holding costs, production costs, capacity absorption, and demand for item i in period t, respectively. Decisions for item i in period t are represented by the production variables $x_{i,t}$, the inventory variables $I_{i,t}$, and the binary setup variables $y_{i,t}$. The objective (2.9) states that total costs are minimized. Furthermore, constraints (2.10) define inventory variables, constraints (2.11) assure that total production, expressed in time units $(b_i x_{i,t})$, does not exceed available capacity (C_t), and constraints (2.12) are the coupling constraints between setup and production variables. Finally, (2.13) represents the non-negativity condition on production and inventory, while (2.14) reflects the binary character of decisions on setups.

Computational complexity and algorithms.

The computational complexity of CLSP has been studied by Florian et al. [42], and by Bitran and Yanasse [17]. These authors consider in their papers the *single item* problem, and prove that the problem is NP-Hard for arbitrary cost functions. However, in case of zero setup costs, or constant setup costs and equal capacities in each period, they show that the problem can be solved efficiently by a dynamic programming algorithm. Moreover, Baker et al. [10] suggest a dynamic programming algorithm for the single item problem with constant costs and arbitrary capacities in each period, while Pochet [89] proposes a solution procedure for the model with a general cost function, based on polyhedral techniques in combination with a branch-and-bound procedure.

The *multi-item* CLSP is NP-Hard (see Chen and Thizy [25]), except for a few special cases (e.g. when all setup costs are zero). The problem is also "hard" in a practical sense, since optimal solution methods have failed to solve all but very small problems within reasonable computation times. It is therefore not surprising that most algorithms are heuristic in nature. Exceptions are found in a few papers. In Barany et al. [11] and Leung et al. [75] exact solution procedures are suggested, based on cut-generation techniques. Additionally, Eppen and Martin [38] use variable redifinition techniques to obtain a stronger model formulation. These "exact" algorithms rely further upon branch-and-bound enumeration to obtain a final optimal solution.

According to the classification of lotsizing heuristics as suggested in Maes and Van Wassenhove [82], approximation methods for CLSP can be divided into *single resource* heuristics and *mathematical program-*

ming based heuristics.

Single resource heuristics are *"greedy"* methods, which usually consist of a *feasibility routine*, and a *priority index*. The feasibility routine guarantees that final production schedules are feasible, while the priority index acts as a cost criterion based on which production capacity in each planning period is distributed among items. A subset of the single resource heuristics plan the production *"period-by-period"*, starting in period 1 and proceeding upto period T, thereby ensuring feasibility during the whole planning process. Heuristics of this type can be found in Eisenhut [35], Lambrecht and Vanderveken [72], Dixon and Silver [30], and Maes and Van Wassenhove [81]. Another category of single resource heuristics are the *"improvement heuristics"*. These heuristics start out with a solution for the complete horizon, thereby disregarding the capacity constraints. Generally, this starting solution will be infeasible. Upon execution of the procedure, feasible production schedules are generated by simple shifting routines. Well-known improvement heuristics are suggested by Dogramaci et al. [33], Karni and Roll [66], and Van Nunen and Wessels [87].

Mathematical programming based heuristics can be subdivided into *relaxation* heuristics, *linear-programming based* heuristics, and *column generation* heuristics. The Lagrangean relaxation heuristic by Thizy and Van Wassenhove [100] is based on relaxation of capacity constraints, in combination with subgradient optimization techniques. An alternative relaxation heuristic, based on relaxation of demand constraints, is discussed in [25].
The linear programming heuristics, suggested by Maes et al. [80], rely on solving the linear programming relaxation of a plant location reformulation of the lotsizing problem. The solution obtained from the LP-relaxation of the model is then rounded-off in different ways to achieve feasible production plans.
Finally, column generation heuristics, based on set-covering or set-partitioning approaches, are discussed by Chen and Thizy [25] and by Cattrysse et al. [23].
For an extensive computational study of the behaviour of the different heuristics, the reader is referred to Maes [79].

Extensions.

The model extension of CLSP, most frequently reported on in literature, considers setup times in addition to setup costs. This model extension changes capacity constraints (2.11) into:

$$\sum_{i=1}^{N}(b_i x_{i,t} + a_i y_{i,t}) \leq C_t \qquad\qquad \text{for } t = 1,..,T \quad (2.11')$$

where a_i is the setup time for item i.

Maes et al. [80] proved that the problem of finding a feasible solution to the set of constraints (2.10), (2.11'), (2.12), (2.13), and (2.14) is NP-Complete. To escape from infeasibility, most heuristics do not consider the original problem formulation, but add possibilities for over-time work against certain costs. Examples of this type of heuristics, usually based on relaxation techniques, are found in Billington et al. [15], Lozano et al. [77], and Trigeiro et al. [101]. The heuristics proposed by Diaby [29] and by Kirca [68] consider the problem with setup times but do not account for setup costs.

Models with backlogging possibilities have been studied by Pochet and Wolsey [90].

Other interesting model extensions, not yet investigated extensively, include problems that deal with multiple capacity constraints in each period, sequence dependent setup costs, and time-dependent production rates. Maes and Van Wassenhove [82] noted that these changes seem subtle at first glance, but may have a considerable effect on problem difficulty.

2.5.3 The Continuous Setup Lotsizing Problem (CSLP)

The Continuous Setup Lotsizing Problem (CSLP) is a problem closely related to CLSP as far as the problem statement is concerned, although two important differences exist. The first difference consists herein, that

for CSLP setup costs are incurred only in the *first* period of an uninterrupted sequence of production periods for the same item ("batch"),
while for CLSP setup costs are incurred in each period that production
takes place for a particular item, even if production for the same item
takes place in two or more consecutive periods. A second difference
between CSLP and CLSP is, that CSLP allows for at most *one* item to
be produced per period, whereas in CLSP no limitations exist with respect to the maximum number of items produced per period. Following
the classification of lotsizing models, as stated earlier in this chapter,
CSLP is categorised as a "small" time bucket model, while CLSP is
categorised as a "large" time bucket model.

Model formulation.

Mathematically, CSLP is formulated as the following mixed-integer program:

CSLP:

$$\min \sum_{i=1}^{N} \sum_{t=1}^{T} \left(S_i \max(0, y_{i,t} - y_{i,t-1}) + h_i I_{i,t} + p_{i,t} x_{i,t} \right) \tag{2.15}$$

subject to

$$I_{i,t-1} + x_{i,t} - d_{i,t} = I_{i,t} \qquad i = 1, .., N; \, t = 1, .., T \tag{2.16}$$

$$\sum_{i=1}^{N} y_{i,t} \leq 1 \qquad t = 1, .., T \tag{2.17}$$

$$b_i x_{i,t} \leq C_{i,t} y_{i,t} \qquad i = 1, .., N; \, t = 1, .., T \tag{2.18}$$

$$x_{i,t}, I_{i,t} \geq 0 \qquad i = 1, .., N; \, t = 1, .., T \tag{2.19}$$

$$y_{i,t} \in \{0, 1\} \qquad i = 1, .., N; \, t = 1, .., T \tag{2.20}$$

where $C_{i,t}$ is the upper bound on production capacity for item i in
period t. The definition for the other symbols, used in this model for-

mulation, is the same as for CLSP.

The objective (minimizing the sum of setup costs, holding costs and production costs) is expressed by (2.15). To explain the setup cost structure, we first define a *batch* of item i as an uninterrupted sequence of periods in which production takes place for item i. Setup costs for item i are incurred in each period t in which a batch starts, which is reflected by the term $S_i \max(0, y_{i,t} - y_{i,t-1})$ in (2.15). The inventory holding costs and the production costs for item i in period t are expressed by the terms $h_i I_{i,t}$ and $p_{i,t} x_{i,t}$, respectively. The set of equations (2.16) assures that the demand $d_{i,t}$ for item i in period t is fulfilled without backlogging, while the set of equations (2.17) guarantees that at most one item is produced per period. Constraints (2.18) state that production for each item-period combination is within bounds set by capacity ($C_{i,t}$). Finally, (2.19) are the non-negativity conditions on production and inventory variables, whereas the binary character of the production variables is expressed by (2.20).

Computational complexity and algorithms.

Although the *single item* CSLP is NP-Hard (see Florian et al. [42]), relatively large problem instances have been solved to optimality within a reasonable amount of time. This may indicate that, at least from a computational point of view, the CSLP formulation is more "tractable" than the formulation for CLSP.

An exact algorithm for the single item problem, based on relaxation of capacity constraints (2.18) in combination with dynamic programming and an enumeration procedure, is discussed by Karmarkar et al. [64].

The *multi-item* problem was first studied by Karmarkar and Schrage [65]. They present a heuristic based on straightforward relaxation of capacity constraints, combined with subgradient optimization. The relaxation heuristic is embedded in a branch-and-bound procedure, to obtain optimal production schedules.

<u>*Extensions.*</u>

So far, two important problem extensions to the generic CSLP, as formulated above, have been proposed in literature. The first one, presented in [65], touches (but does not solve) the CSLP problem with sequence-dependent setup costs. The second problem extension, suggested by de Matta and Guignard [85], considers the CSLP with parallel machines and sequence independent setup costs. The authors propose a heuristic, which relies upon the combination of a greedy algorithm, and Lagrange-relaxation.

2.5.4 The Discrete Lotsizing and Scheduling Problem (DLSP).

The generic formulation of the Discrete Lotsizing and Scheduling Problem (DLSP) is to a large extent similar to the generic formulation for CSLP, in that it also assumes at most one item to be produced per period, as well as batch setup costs. The only difference between the two model formulations consists herein, that in DLSP the quantity produced in each period is either assumed to be zero, *or* equal to the full production capacity. Models of this type are often called *"all or nothing production"* models in literature.

<u>*Model formulation.*</u>

The generic version of the Discrete Lotsizing and Scheduling Problem (DLSP) was suggested in 1988 by Fleischmann [40], and can be formulated as the following mixed-integer program:

Generic DLSP:

$$\min \sum_{i=1}^{N} \sum_{t=1}^{T} \left(S_i \max(0, y_{i,t} - y_{i,t-1}) + h_i I_{i,t} + p'_{i,t} y_{i,t} \right) \qquad (2.21)$$

subject to

$$I_{i,t-1} + r_i y_{i,t} - d_{i,t} = I_{i,t} \qquad\qquad i = 1, ..N; t = 1, .., T \quad (2.22)$$

$$\sum_{i=1}^{N} y_{i,t} \leq 1 \qquad\qquad t = 1, .., T \qquad\qquad (2.23)$$

$$I_{i,t} \geq 0 \qquad\qquad i = 1, .., N; t = 1, .., T \quad (2.24)$$

$$y_{i,t} \in \{0, 1\} \qquad\qquad i = 1, .., N; t = 1, .., T \quad (2.25)$$

The notation used in this model formulation, as well as the interpretation of constraints, is analogous to CSLP. Mathematically, the difference between the two models is represented by the absence of production variables $x_{i,t}$ and constraints (2.18) in DLSP. This is feasible, since "all or nothing production" implies that $x_{i,t} = r_i y_{i,t}$. It should be noted that, as an immediate consequence of this substitution, the term $p_{i,t} x_{i,t}$ in the objective function (2.15) of CLSP has changed into $p'_{i,t} y_{i,t}$ in (2.21) of DLSP (of course, $p'_{i,t} = p_{i,t} r_i$).
As we will see in subsequent chapters, the above model formulation for DLSP can be further simplified, by linearization of the objective function, and by elimination of inventory variables $I_{i,t}$.

Since the Discrete Lotsizing and Scheduling Problem is subject to discussion in Chapters 3,4, and 5, the reader is referred to these chapters for an overview on computational complexity, algorithms, and possible problem extensions.

2.6 Summary and discussion

In this chapter we considered a framework for mathematical formulations of production planning problems, due to [55]. Applying some simplifications to this general framework yields a METAMODEL, which contains the most important building blocks used in lotsizing models, like e.g. cost functions, demand functions, production functions, and capacity constraints. After a thorough discussion of these building blocks, we focused on a number of specific formulations for lotsizing problems. Thereby, differentiation was made between formulations for *uncapacitated* lotsizing problems, like the EOQ-model, and the Wagner-Whitin model, and formulations for *capacitated* lotsizing problems, like ELSP, CLSP, CSLP, and DLSP. In Table 2.2 we summarize a number of the most important similarities and dissimilarities between the model formulations considered in this chapter.

Table 2.2. Comparison between lotsizing models.

	time axis	maximum # of items produced per period	setup cost	demand	production quantity per period
EOQ	infinite, continuous	1	constant, per batch	constant	unrestricted
WW	finite, discrete	1	dynamic, per period	dynamic	unrestricted
ELSP	infinite, continuous	(1	constant, per batch	constant	(2
CLSP	finite, discrete	unrestricted	dynamic, per period	dynamic	less than or equal to capacity
CSLP	finite, discrete	1	dynamic, per batch	dynamic	less than or equal to capacity
DLSP	finite, discrete	1	dynamic, per batch	dynamic	zero or equal to capacity

(^{1} Maximum production of one item *per unit of time*.
(^{2} Production quantity equal to zero or equal to production rate.

Chapter 3

The Discrete Lotsizing and Scheduling Problem (DLSP)

3.1 Introduction

In this chapter we consider some extensions and generalizations of the Discrete Lotsizing and Scheduling Problem (DLSP), introduced in Chapter 2. These extensions and generalizations may prove useful in practice, and include problems with sequence dependent setup costs, problems with sequence dependent setup times, and parallel machine problems. Moreover, for all problems defined in this chapter, *computational complexity* results are derived. These results do not only provide an interesting theoretical insight in the "hardness" of the DLSP problem, but may also serve as a good indicator for the computational behaviour of algorithms.

The remainder of this chapter is organized as follows: In Section 3.2 we introduce a standard problem notation which identifies the various DLSP problems, and in Section 3.3 results on computational complexity are derived for all DLSP problems defined by our standard problem notation. Finally, Section 3.4 concludes this chapter with a summary.

3.2   Standard problem notation

To describe the problem variants of DLSP considered here, we introduce the following six field notation:

$$L/M/N/SC/PC/ST$$

The specific problem characteristics represented in this notation are discussed below:

- Layout of the production line *(field identifier: L)*. In the problems that will be considered in this chapter, production takes place at one or more *Parallel* machines. The production rate of each parallel machine is denoted by constants $r_{i,m}$, where i ranges over all item numbers, and m ranges over all machine numbers. The parallel machines are *Identical* (PI), when the production rate is machine independent, that is, when $r_{i,m}$ is independent of m, for all items i. The parallel machines are *Uniform* (PU), when the production rate is machine dependent, but differs only in a constant C_m, that is $r_{i,m} = C_m r_i$. In all other cases the machines are called *Unrelated* (P). When only one machine is considered, this field is omitted.

- The number of machines. *(field identifier M)*. If the number of machines is not part of the problem description (as will be assumed at certain points when addressing questions concerning computational complexity), this is denoted by an asterisk (*).

- The number of items *(field identifier: N)*. When the number of items is not part of the problem description, this is denoted by an asterisk (*).

- The setup cost structure *(field identifier: SC)*. In the generic version of the DLSP, the setup costs are assumed to be *Sequence Independent* (SI) implying that the setup cost for a batch of item i, S_i, does not depend on the preceding batch. If, on the other hand, the setup costs for a batch of item i depend on the preceding batch, consisting, say, of item j, then setup costs are *Sequence*

Dependent (SD), and setup costs for a changeover from item j to item i are denoted by $S_{j,i}$. Moreover, in Chapter 4 problems are considered with *Time Dependent* (TD) setup costs. Finally, if all setup costs are zero, this is denoted by *A (Absent)* in the six field notation.

- The production cost structure *(field identifier: PC)*. The production costs $p_{i,t}$ may be *Constant* over time (C), that is, for each item i, $p_{i,t}$ does not depend on the period t. In all other cases the production costs are *General* (G).

- The setup time structure *(field identifier: ST)*. The symbol A (absent) denotes zero setup times. In case of sequence independency (SI), the setup time (a_i) for a batch of item i only depends on i and not on preceding batches. If setup times are sequence dependent (SD), a switch from production of item j to production of item i requires a setup time $(a_{j,i})$, which depends on both j and i.

In Table 3.1 all possible values for each field in the six field notation are summarized.

Table 3.1. Six field notation for DLSP.		
contents	*field*	*range*
layout of production line[1	L	Parallel Identical (PI)
		Parallel Uniform (PU)
		Parallel Unrelated (P)
number of machines	M	positive integer or *
number of items	N	positive integer or *
setup cost structure	SC	Absent (A)
		Sequence Independent (SI)
		Sequence Dependent (SD)
		Time Dependent (TD)
production cost structure	PC	Constant (C)
		General (G)
setup time structure	ST	Absent (A)
		Sequence Independent (SI)
		Sequence Dependent (SD)
[1 This field is omitted for one machine problems.		

Subsequently, when a particular field takes any fixed value from the range, considered as part of the problem description and not as (variable) input to the problem, the corresponding field identifier will be used explicitly.

To conclude this section, we demonstrate the use of our six field notation by the following examples:

Examples:

1. The notation $1/N/SI/G/A$ describes the generic DLSP, formulated in Chapter 2. (Note that the first field is left out, as the one machine case is considered)

2. The generic DLSP in which the number of items is not fixed beforehand, i.e., is not part of the problem description, is denoted by $1/*/SI/G/A$.

3. The notation $P/*/N/SC/PC/ST$ identifies the unrelated parallel machine problem in which the number of machines is not regarded as prespecified, that is, not as part of the problem description.

3.3   Complexity results

In this section we derive *computational complexity* results for various DLSP problems. For the reader, not familiar with this subject, an introduction to the theory of computational complexity is given by Garey and Johnson [44].

In our analysis of the computational complexity of DLSP problems, we differentiate between *feasibility* problems, which will be considered in Section 3.3.1, and *optimization* problems, to be considered in Section 3.3.2.

In what follows the feasibility problem for a given DLSP variant $L/M/N/SC/PC/ST$ is denoted by $(L/M/N/SC/PC/ST)_F$, while the optimization problem is simply denoted by $L/M/N/SC/PC/ST$.

3.3.1 Feasibility problems

The feasibility problem is to determine whether a production schedule exists wherein demand for all items is fulfilled without backlogging and capacity constraints are not violated. Subsequently, we analyse the feasibility problem for the one machine case and for parallel machines.

One machine problems.

Mathematically, the feasibility problem for the one machine DLSP can be stated as: Does there exist a feasible solution to the following set of equations:

$$\sum_{\tau=1}^{t} y_{i,\tau} \geq D_{i,t} \qquad\qquad i = 1,..,N;\ t = 1,..,T-1 \quad (3.1a)$$

$$\sum_{\tau=1}^{T} y_{i,\tau} = D_{i,T} \qquad\qquad i = 1,..,N \qquad\qquad (3.1b)$$

$$\sum_{i=1}^{N} y_{i,t} + \sum_{i\in\mathcal{A}} v_{i,t} \leq 1 \qquad\qquad t = 1,..,T \qquad\qquad (3.2)$$

$$v_{i,t-a_i+\tau} \geq y_{i,t} - y_{i,t-1} \qquad i \in \mathcal{A};\ t = a_i+1,..,T; \qquad (3.3)$$
$$\tau = 0,..,a_i-1$$

$$y_{i,t}, v_{i,t} \in \{0,1\} \qquad\qquad i = 1,..,N;\ t = 1,..,T \qquad (3.4)$$

where N is the number of items, T is the number of planning periods, and a_i is the (integer) setup time for item i, expressed in periods. The set $\mathcal{A}$ is defined as the set of item numbers with positive setup time, thus $\mathcal{A} = \{i \mid a_i > 0\}$. Furthermore, constants $D_{i,t}$ are defined as the *normalized* cumulative demand for item i up to period t, i.e. demand expressed as the (integer) number of required production periods:

$$D_{i,t} = \max(0, \lceil (\sum_{\tau=1}^{t} d_{i,\tau} - I_{i,0})/r_i \rceil) \qquad\qquad (3.5)$$

with $\lceil x \rceil$ the smallest integer greater than or equal to x.

Decision variables in the model are $v_{i,t}$ $(y_{i,t})$, which are equal to one when the machine is in setup (production) for item i in period t, and zero otherwise. The set of equations (3.1a) and (3.1b) assure that cumulative production up to period t is large enough to fulfil cumulative demand, expressed in terms of required production periods. The equations (3.2) guarantee that in each planning period the machine is either in production, or in setup, or idle. The coupling between setup $(v_{i,t})$ and production variables $(y_{i,t})$ is expressed by the equations (3.3). Here, it is assumed that these variables are prespecified for $t \leq 0$. Finally, the set of equations (3.4) represent integrality conditions on setup and production variables.

For DLSP wherein all setup times are zero, the feasibility problem can be solved efficiently by checking whether available capacity up to period t is sufficient to accommodate total demand up to period t, i.e.

$$\sum_{i=1}^{N} D_{i,t} \leq t \qquad\qquad\qquad \text{for } t = 1,..,T \quad (3.6)$$

When setup times are nonzero feasibility cannot be verified using (3.6), since the number of setups for each item (and therefore the total setup time) is unknown beforehand. In this section it will be shown that the feasibility problem is NP-Complete when setup times are nonzero.

In the proofs below, the following definitions and notations will be used:

Definition: A *deadline* is a period in which a positive demand occurs. The number of deadlines for item i is denoted by DL_i and the period wherein the n-th deadline occurs is denoted by $t_{i,n}$, for $n = 0,..,DL_i+1$ (for practical purposes we set $t_{i,0} = 0$ and $t_{i,DL_i+1} = T+1$). In addition, we define the ordered set $\mathcal{D}_i$ as the set of deadlines for item i. Thus, $\mathcal{D}_i = \{0\} \cup \{t \mid d_{i,t} > 0\} \cup \{T+1\}$.
□

Furthermore, to introduce the difference between *non-preemptive* and *preemptive* DLSP schedules, let $y = \{y_{i,t}\}_{all\ i,t}$ be a feasible schedule for the DLSP and let $L_i(y)$ be the set of periods in which a production batch ends and cumulative production is not equal to any occurring cumulative demand, that is:

$$L_i(y) = \left\{ t \mid y_{i,t} - y_{i,t+1} = 1 \wedge \left(\sum_{\tau=1}^{t} y_{i,\tau} \neq D_{i,t_{i,n}} \text{ for } n = 1, .., DL_i \right) \right\}$$

Definition: A DLSP schedule y is called *non-preemptive* if $L_i(y) = \emptyset$ for $i = 1, .., N$. Otherwise, the schedule is called *preemptive*.
□

Lemma 3.1 *Every preemptive feasible schedule $y = \{y_{i,t}\}_{all\ i,t}$ for problem $1/N/SC/G/SI$ can be transformed into a feasible non preemptive schedule $y^\star = \{y_{i,t}^\star\}_{all\ i,t}$ in polynomial time. Furthermore, the number of setups made for schedule $y^\star$ is not greater than for schedule y.*

Proof: For an arbitrary item i and an arbitrary deadline $n(= 0, .., DL_i - 1)$, let $\tilde{t}_1$ be the first period t for which $\sum_{\tau=1}^{t} y_{i,\tau} = D_{i,t_{i,n+1}}$. Determine $\tilde{t}_0$ as the first period t for which $\sum_{\tau=1}^{t} y_{i,\tau} > D_{i,t_{i,n}}$. Note that in the interval $[\tilde{t}_0, \tilde{t}_1]$ production takes place during $q = D_{i,t_{i,n+1}} - D_{i,t_{i,n}}$ periods. All $t \in L_i(y)$ which may exist in the interval $[\tilde{t}_0, \tilde{t}_1 - 1]$ can be eliminated without creating additional setups by replanning the production of q to occur in the interval $[\tilde{t}_1 - q + 1, \tilde{t}_1]$ and feasibility is maintained by, if necessary, shifting production of items $j(\neq i)$ to earlier periods. The latter is also done without creating additional setups.
Call the resulting schedule y'. Now, it is clear that $L_i(y') = L_i(y) \setminus \{t \mid t \in [\tilde{t}_0, \tilde{t}_1]\}$. Furthermore $L_j(y') \subseteq L_j(y)$ for all items $j = 1, .., N$. Proceeding in this way, ultimately a schedule $y^\star$ results for which $L_i(y^\star) = \emptyset$ for $i = 1, .., N$. Since the number of deadlines is bounded by T, and since finding a pair $(\tilde{t}_0, \tilde{t}_1)$ can be done in $\mathcal{O}(T)$, the algorithm runs in $\mathcal{O}(T^2)$.
□

In Theorem 3.1 we prove that problem $(1/*/A/G/SI)_F$ is NP-Complete. The proof of this theorem uses a reduction from the Job Class Scheduling Problem $(JCSP)$ considered by Bruno and Downey [20]. This problem can be formulated as follows:

JCSP:

Suppose J jobs are given which have to be carried out on a single machine. The attributes of job j are: an integer processing time β_j, a deadline δ_j, and a job class γ_j. The number of different job classes is equal to Γ. If a job does *not immediately* follow another job of the same job class, then a machine setup is required before processing of the job can start. Such a setup takes 1 time unit.

The question to be answered in *JCSP* is whether there exists a *non preemptive* schedule in which none of the jobs finishes after its deadline. In [20] Bruno and Downey prove that *JCSP* is NP-Complete.

Theorem 3.1 *Problem $(1/*/A/C/SI)_F$ is NP-Complete, even if all the setup times are equal to 1.*

Proof: We show that $JCSP \propto (1/*/A/C/SI)_F$. Let I_1 be an instance of *JCSP* with attributes as described above. Then an instance I_2 of $(1/*/A/C/SI)_F$ can be constructed as follows:

- Each item in I_2 corresponds to a job class in I_1. Hence the number of items is equal to Γ.

- The set of deadlines for an item in I_2 is equal to the set of deadlines of the jobs in the corresponding job class in I_1.

- $D_{i,t_{i,n}} = \sum_{j \in J_{i,n}} \beta_j$ for $i = 1, .., \Gamma$ and $n = 1, .., 3$. Here the set of jobs $J_{i,n}$ is defined as: $J_{i,n} = \{j | \gamma_j = i \text{ and } \delta_j \leq t_{i,n}\}$.

- $a_i = 1$ for $i = 1, .., \Gamma$.

It remains to be shown that I_1 is a yes-instance if and only if I_2 is a yes-instance. It is clear that any feasible schedule for I_1 can be interpreted as a feasible schedule for I_2. This proves the 'only-if' part of the statement.
Unfortunately, a feasible schedule for I_2 may be preemptive and consequently this schedule is not feasible for I_1, since *JCSP* only allows

non preemptive schedules. However, Lemma 3.1 shows that any feasible schedule for I_2 can be transformed into a feasible non preemptive schedule for I_2 in polynomial time. This feasible non preemptive schedule for I_2 can be interpreted as a feasible schedule for I_1, which proves the 'if' part of the statement. Since $JCSP$ is NP-Complete and since it is obvious that $(1/*/A/G/SI)_F$ is in $\mathcal{NP}$, it follows that $(1/*/A/G/SI)_F$ is NP-Complete.
□

Parallel machine problems.

The feasibility problem for parallel machine systems with zero setup times can be stated mathematically as: Does there exist a feasible solution to the following set of equations:

$$\sum_{\tau=1}^{t}\sum_{m=1}^{M} r_{i,m} y_{i,\tau,m} \geq \sum_{\tau=1}^{t} d_{i,\tau} \qquad i = 1,..,N; t = 1,..,T \qquad (3.7)$$

$$\sum_{i=1}^{N} y_{i,t,m} \leq 1 \qquad t = 1,..,T; m = 1,..,M \qquad (3.8)$$

$$y_{i,t,m} \in \{0,1\} \qquad \begin{aligned} i &= 1,..,N; t = 1,..,T; \\ m &= 1,..,M \end{aligned} \qquad (3.9)$$

where N is the number of items, M is the number of machines, and T is the number of periods. Furthermore, $r_{i,m}$ is the production rate for item i at machine m, and $d_{i,t}$ is the demand for item i in period t. Decision variables $y_{i,t,m}$ are equal to one if item i is produced in period t at machine m, and zero otherwise. Constraints (3.7) state that cumulative production for item i is at least equal to cumulative demand in each period t, while (3.8) assures that for each period-machine combination at most one item is produced. Finally, (3.9) state that production variables are binary.

In case of identical machines, feasibility can be checked efficiently by an adapted version of the set of equations (3.6), i.e.,

$$\sum_{i=1}^{N} D_{i,t} \le Mt \qquad\qquad\qquad \text{for } t = 1, .., T. \quad (3.6')$$

However, if the machines are uniform, constants $D_{i,t}$ cannot be computed anymore, since the production rate is machine dependent. We will show that in this case the feasibility problem is NP-Complete, and consequently, it is unlikely that an efficient check like (3.6') exists.
The proof is based on the Set Partitioning Problem (SPP), which can be stated as follows:

SPP:

Given J positive integers $\tau_1, \tau_2, ..., \tau_J$ and an integer K, such that $\sum_i \tau_i = 2K$. Does there exist a set $I \subset \{1, .., J\}$ for which:

$$\sum_{i \in I} \tau_i = \sum_{i \notin I} \tau_i \; ?$$

It is well known, that SPP is NP-Complete (see e.g. Garey and Johnson [44]).

Theorem 3.2 *Problem* $(PU/*/2/A/C/A)_F$ *is NP-Complete.*

Proof: We show that $SPP \propto (PU/*/2/A/C/A)_F$. Let I_1 be an instance of SPP with attributes as described above. Then an instance I_2 of $(PU/*/2/A/C/A)_F$ can be constructed as follows:

The number of periods (T) is equal to 1.

The number of machines (M) is equal to J.

$C_m = \tau_m$ for $m = 1, .., M$.

$r_i = 1$ for $i = 1, 2$.

$D_{1,1} = D_{2,1} = K$.

Suppose a feasible solution exists for I_2. Then, by taking the set I as:

$$I = \{ \text{ all machine numbers which produce for item 1 } \},$$

it is clear that I is a solution to I_1. On the other hand, it is also clear that any solution to I_1 can be transformed into a feasible solution to I_2.

Since SPP is NP-Complete, and since $(PU/*/2/A/C/A)_F$ clearly belongs to $\mathcal{NP}$, it follows that $(PU/*/2/A/C/A)_F$ is NP-Complete.
□

A few remarks can be made with respect to this complexity result. First, it is obvious that the feasibility problem for unrelated machines is also NP-Complete, since uniform machines are a special case of unrelated machines. Secondly, it is clear that a feasible schedule for the single item problem can be obtained in polynomial time, by scheduling demand period by period at the fastest available machine not yet used. We conclude this discussion with a reference to Section 3.3.2, where an efficient algorithm is presented for a special case of unrelated machines for which $r_{i,m} \in \{0, r_i\}$ for all $i = 1, .., N$ and $m = 1, .., M$.

3.3.2 Optimization problems

The optimization problem is the problem of finding a *feasible* production schedule with *minimal total costs*. We restrict our analysis to those problems for which the feasibility problem is solvable in polynomial time, since it is obvious that NP-Completeness of the feasibility problem implies NP-Hardness of the corresponding optimization problem. Consequently, we consider only the single machine problem with nonzero setup costs, and the parallel identical machine problem with zero setup costs.

The single machine problem with nonzero setup costs.

Mathematically, the single machine optimization problem with nonzero setup costs is the problem of determining a production schedule which satisfies the conditions (2.21) to (2.25). The complexity of this problem, which is denoted by 1/*/SI/C/A when production costs are constant over time, is stated by the following theorem.

Theorem 3.3 *Problem 1/*/SI/C/A is NP-Hard.*

Proof: We show that $SPP \propto 1/*/SI/C/A$. Let I_1 be an instance of SPP. Consider the following instance I_2 of $1/*/SI/C/A$:

The number of periods (T) is equal to $2K + 1$.

The number of items (N) is equal to $J + 1$.

$S_i = 1$ for $i = 1, .., N$.

$h_i = 0$ for $i = 1, .., N - 1$.

$h_N = 1$.

$p_{i,t} = 0$ for $i = 1, .., N$ and $t = 1, .., T$

$r_i = 1$ for $i = 1, .., N$

$$d_{i,t} = \begin{cases} \tau_i & \text{for } i = 1, .., N-1 \text{ and } t = 2K+1 \\ 1 & \text{for } i = N \text{ and } t = K+1 \\ 0 & \text{otherwise} \end{cases}$$

Now we prove that I_1 is a yes-instance if and only if the optimal solution to I_2 has total costs equal to N. Therefore, suppose a solution with total costs equal to N exists for I_2. Since there is a deadline for each item, at least N setups must be made in any feasible solution. A solution with total costs equal to N must therefore have no holding costs. Hence, demand for item N is produced in period $K + 1$ and there is exactly one setup for all other items. Some of these items are produced in periods 1 to K and others in periods $K + 2$ to $2K + 1$.
Now it is clear that if the set I is defined as:

$$I = \{ \text{ all item numbers produced in the periods 1 to } K \}$$

then I is a solution to I_1. On the other hand, any solution to I_1 can be transformed into a solution to I_2, with total cost equal to N. From the above it follows that any solution technique for $1/*/SI/C/A$ can be used as a solution technique for SPP. Since SPP is NP-Complete,

it follows that the optimization problem $1/*/SI/C/A$ is NP-Hard.
□

The parallel identical machine problem with zero setup costs.

In Theorem 3.4 below we state the computational complexity of the parallel identical machine problem with zero setup costs, which is denoted by $PI/M/N/A/G/A$.

Theorem 3.4 _Problem $PI/M/N/A/G/A$ is polynomially solvable._

Proof: The reader may verify that $PI/M/N/A/G/A$ can be formulated as a transportation problem. Since it is well-known that the transportation problem is solvable in polynomial time, $PI/M/N/A/G/A$ is solvable in polynomial time too.
□

With respect to this complexity result two remarks can be made. First, it can easily be seen that the special case of problem $P/M/N/A/G/A$ for which $r_{i,m} \in \{0, r_i\}$ for all $i = 1, .., N$ and $m = 1, .., M$ can also be formulated as a transportation problem. Consequently, this problem can also be solved in polynomial time. Secondly, as will be shown in Appendix A of this chapter, $PI/M/N/A/C/A$ can be solved in a _greedy_ fashion using the following _column minima_ procedure:

COLUMN MINIMA PROCEDURE:

Step 0: Sort and renumber all items such that $r_1 h_1 \geq r_2 h_2 \geq ... \geq r_N h_N$.

Step 1: Schedule for the lowest numbered item i, not yet considered, all demand as late as possible.

Step 2: Update the available capacity and repeat step 1 until all demand is scheduled for all items.

The reader may verify that the running time of this procedure is $\mathcal{O}(N \log N + NT)$.

Finally, a variant of $PI/M/N/A/G/A$ is considered. In this variant, each item i may be produced in period t by at most $R_{i,t}(\leq M)$ machines. This is for instance the case when a limited number $R_{i,t}$ of molds are available for each item i in period t. In what follows, we call this problem the *restricted resource* problem, denote as $(PI/M/N/A/G/A)^R$. Mathematically, it is formulated as:

$$\min \sum_{i=1}^{N} \sum_{t=1}^{T} \sum_{m=1}^{M} (h_i I_{i,t} + p_{i,t} y_{i,t,m}) \tag{3.10}$$

subject to

$$\sum_{m=1}^{M} y_{i,t,m} \leq R_{i,t} \qquad\qquad i = 1, .., N; \, t = 1, .., T \tag{3.11}$$

(3.7), (3.8), (3.9)

where the objective (3.10) states that total costs are minimized, and (3.11) assures that for each item-period combination at most $R_{i,t}(\leq M)$ units are produced.

Theorem 3.5 *Problem* $(PI/M/N/A/G/A)^R$ *is polynomially solvable.*

Proof: Problem $(PI/M/N/A/G/A)^R$ can be reformulated in terms of the variables $z_{i,t}$, which denote the integer number of machines producing for item i in period t. Before we state the constraints of the reformulated problem, we introduce the following notation:

- $A = \{\delta_{i,j}\}_{i,j=1,..,T}$ such that $\delta_{i,j} = 1$ if $i \leq j$ and zero otherwise,

- E is the identity matrix with dimension T,

- $\overline{Z} = (z_{1,1}, .., z_{1,T}, .., .., z_{N,1}, .., z_{N,T})'$,

- $\overline{D}_k = (D_{k,1}, .., D_{k,T})'$,

- $\overline{M} = (M, .., .., M)'$,

- $\overline{R}_k = (R_{k,1}, .., R_{k,T})'$.

In matrix notation, the constraints of the reformulated problem are stated as:

$$
\begin{pmatrix}
A & & & & \emptyset \\
 & \ddots & & & \\
 & & \ddots & & \\
\emptyset & & & A & \\
E & \cdots & \cdots & E \\
E & & & \emptyset \\
 & \ddots & & & \\
 & & \ddots & & \\
 & & & \emptyset & E
\end{pmatrix}
\overline{Z}
\begin{pmatrix}
\geq \\
\vdots \\
\vdots \\
\geq \\
\leq \\
\leq \\
\vdots \\
\vdots \\
\leq
\end{pmatrix}
\begin{pmatrix}
\overline{D}_1 \\
\vdots \\
\vdots \\
\overline{D}_N \\
\overline{M} \\
\overline{R}_1 \\
\vdots \\
\vdots \\
\overline{R}_N
\end{pmatrix}
$$

The above coefficient matrix is *totally unimodular*, which can be shown as follows: Consider a coefficient matrix B, which is formed by (a number of) coefficients from matrices A and (a number of) coefficients from matrices E, multiplied by -1 (see below).

$$
B = \begin{pmatrix}
1 & 1 & 0 & 0 & 0 & 0 \\
1 & 1 & 1 & 0 & 0 & 0 \\
0 & 0 & 0 & 1 & 1 & 0 \\
0 & 0 & 0 & 1 & 1 & 1 \\
0 & -1 & 0 & 0 & -1 & 0 \\
0 & 0 & -1 & 0 & 0 & -1
\end{pmatrix}
\qquad
B' = \begin{pmatrix}
1 & 1 & 0 & 0 & 0 & 0 \\
0 & 0 & 1 & 0 & 0 & 0 \\
0 & 0 & 0 & 1 & 1 & 0 \\
0 & 0 & 0 & 0 & 0 & 1 \\
0 & -1 & 0 & 0 & -1 & 0 \\
0 & 0 & -1 & 0 & 0 & -1
\end{pmatrix}
$$

Each column of a square submatrix of the matrix B can be reduced by elementary row operations to a column that contains at most one element equal to $+1$ and at most one element equal to -1 (matrix B' above). If the column contains only one element equal to $+1$ or -1, the submatrix can be developed along this column and the determinant of the resulting submatrix is multiplied by $+1$ or -1. This is repeated until a matrix arises that contains exactly one element equal to $+1$ and exactly one element equal to -1 in each column. This matrix is the incidence-matrix of a directed network, and hence it has determinant $+1$, -1 or 0 (see Gondran and Minoux [50]). Consequently, an optimal (integer) solution to this problem can be obtained in polynomial time by Linear Programming, using for example Karmarkar's [63] or Khachian's algorithm [67].

$\square$

3.4   Summary and discussion

In this chapter several extensions of the Discrete Lotsizing and Scheduling Problem (DLSP) have been considered. These extensions include problems with non-zero setup times, sequence dependent setup costs and sequence dependent setup times for single- as well as for parallel machine problems.

Complexity results are derived, which show that multi-item single machine problems in which non-zero setup times and/or setup costs occur are NP-Hard, while parallel machine problems are NP-Hard as soon as production speeds are machine-dependent. The identical parallel machine problem with zero setup costs and zero setup times can be solved in polynomial time, even if additional restrictions are imposed on the availability of the machines.

Table 3.2 summarizes the complexity results derived in this chapter.

Table 3.2. Complexity results for DLSP.		
problem	*feasibility problem*	*optimization problem*
PU/*/2/A/G/A P/*/2/A/G/A	NP-Complete[1	NP-Hard
PI/M/N/A/G/A	Polynomially solvable	Polynomially solvable[2
1/*/SI/G/A	Polynomially solvable	NP-Hard[3
1/*/A/G/SI	NP-Complete	NP-Hard
[1 If $r_{i,m} \in \{0, r_i\}$ the problem is polynomially solvable [2 Even the "restricted resource" problem is polynomially solvable [3 Even problem 1/*/SI/C/A is NP-Hard.		

Appendix A

We prove that the column minima method as defined in Section 3.3.2 always leads to an optimal solution for problem $PI/M/N/A/C/A$, if one exists.

The N-item problem $PI/M/N/A/C/A$ can be formulated as an integer linear program (ILP_N). Since production costs are assumed to be time independent, they are omitted from the model formulation. Without loss of generality, the production speed for each item is assumed to equal one.

ILP_N:

$$\min \sum_{i=1}^{N} h_i \sum_{t=1}^{T} \sum_{\tau=1}^{t} (z_{i,\tau} - d_{i,\tau}) \tag{3.12}$$

subject to

$$\sum_{i=1}^{N} z_{i,t} \leq M \qquad\qquad t = 1,..,T \tag{3.13}$$

$$\sum_{\tau=1}^{t} z_{i,\tau} \geq D_{i,t} \qquad\qquad i = 1,..,N; \, t = 1,..,T \tag{3.14}$$

$$z_{i,t} \in \{0, 1, .., M\} \qquad\qquad i = 1,..,N; \, t = 1,..,T \tag{3.15}$$

where $z_{i,t}$ is the (integer) number of machines producing item i in period t.

In what follows it is assumed that a feasible solution for ILP_N exists and that the items are numbered such that $h_1 \geq h_2 \geq h_3 \geq ... \geq h_N$.

Lemma 3.2 *There exists an optimal solution $\{z_{i,t}\}_{i,t}$ to ILP_N, such that $\{z_{1,t}\}_t$ is an optimal solution to ILP_1.*

Proof: Let $\{z^*_{i,t}\}$ be an optimal solution for ILP_N. Now there are two possibilities: Either $\{z^*_{1,t}\}$ is optimal to ILP_1 and the proof is finished, or $\{z^*_{1,t}\}$ is not optimal to ILP_1. For the latter case $\{z^*_{i,t}\}$ can be modified, such that an optimal solution results for ILP_N as well as for ILP_1. To do so, let $\{z'_t\}$ be an optimal solution for ILP_1 and let v be the first period t for which $z'_t \leq z^*_{1,t} - 1$. Furthermore, let $w(> v)$ be the first period t for which $z'_t \geq z^*_{1,t} + 1$.

Define Δz as:

$$\Delta z = \min\{z^*_{1,v} - z_v, z_w - z^*_{1,w}\}$$

Shifting an amount of Δz units of item 1 from period v to period w may cause an infeasible solution for ILP_N. Feasibility can be restored by moving Δz units for one of the items $2, .., N$ from period w to period v. The latter two movements create a change in cost per unit of at most:

$$[\max_{i=2,..,N} h_i](w - v) - h_1(w - v) \leq h_1(w - v) - h_1(w - v) = 0$$

and consequently the new solution is again feasible and optimal for ILP_N. This procedure is repeated a finite number of times, until no periods v and w can be found. The resulting solution satisfies the assertion in the lemma.

□

The lemma demonstrates that an optimal solution for problem ILP_N can be found by first solving problem ILP_1 to optimality, then updating the available capacity and solving the problem for item 2 to optimality, updating the available capacity, and repeating this, until all items are scheduled. This is exactly how the algorithm in Section 3.3.2 works, and consequently this algorithm will always lead to an optimal solution, if one exists.

Chapter 4

The Single Item DLSP

4.1 Introduction

In this chapter we consider the single item Discrete Lotsizing and
Scheduling Problems (DLSP) with general cost structures and zero
setup times. This problem is denoted by 1/1/TD/G/A in the standard problem notation, introduced in Chapter 3.
Recently, several authors have worked on solution procedures for
1/1/TD/G/A, mainly because of its importance when developing decomposition algorithms for multi-item problems (see also Chapter 5).
For instance, Van Wassenhove and Vanderhenst [103] discuss a hierarchical production planning problem in which 1/1/TD/G/A appeared
as a subproblem. They solve the problem by a straightforward dynamic programming (DP) algorithm. Moreover, Magnanti and Vachani
[83] study a problem closely related to the single item DLSP, and
suggest an algorithm based on polyhedral methods in combination
with a branch-and-bound routine. Finally, Lasdon and Terjung [74],
Fleischmann [40] and Cattrysse et al. [24] use dynamic programming
to solve the single item subproblems in their decomposition algorithms
for PI/M/N/SI/C/A, 1/N/SI/G/A and 1/N/SI/G/SI respectively.

The remainder of this chapter is organized as follows. In Section 4.2
we formulate 1/1/TD/G/A as an integer program, and we describe a
set of *valid inequalities* which can be added to the linear programming

relaxation of the integer program, to obtain stronger lower bounds. In addition, a straightforward DP-algorithm is presented to solve DLSP problems with arbitrary cost coefficients in the objective function.

A second procedure to solve $1/1/TD/G/A$, described in Section 4.3, is based on a reformulation of DLSP as an assignment problem, with additional restrictions to reflect the specific (setup) cost structure. For this linear programming formulation it is shown that every extremal optimal solution is all-integer under some additional conditions on the input parameters. In Section 4.4 a third procedure is presented, which is based on a special purpose DP-approach by Kuik, Salomon, Van Hoesel and Van Wassenhove [70]. Using some important properties of optimal solutions, this algorithm can be made to run very fast, provided that some additional restrictions on input parameters are fulfilled. Finally, Section 4.5 concludes this chapter with a summary and a brief discussion of the results.

4.2   Problem formulation

Mathematically, the single-item DLSP can be formulated as the following integer program:

$1/1/TD/G/A$:

$$Z_{DLSP} = \min \sum_{t=1}^{T}(S_t v_t + (h_{t,T} + p_t)y_t - h_t D_t) \qquad (4.1)$$

subject to

$$\sum_{\tau=1}^{t} y_\tau \geq D_t \qquad\qquad t = 1,\ldots,T-1 \quad (4.2a)$$

$$\sum_{\tau=1}^{T} y_\tau = D_T \qquad\qquad (4.2b)$$

$$v_t \geq y_t - y_{t-1} \qquad\qquad t = 1,\ldots,T \qquad (4.3)$$

$$y_t, v_t \in \{0,1\} \qquad\qquad t = 1,\ldots,T \qquad (4.4)$$

where T is the number of planning periods. Moreover, constants S_t, $h_{t,T}$, p_t and D_t are the setup costs in period t, the cumulative holding cost from period t upto period T (we define $h_{\tilde{t}_1,\tilde{t}_2} = \sum_{\tau=\tilde{t}_1}^{\tilde{t}_2} h_\tau$), the production cost in period t, and the cumulative demand upto period t, respectively. The binary decision variables v_t (y_t) are equal to one if period t is a setup (production) period, and zero otherwise. The objective (4.1) is to minimize total costs. It should be noted that inventory variables in each period t (I_t) have been eliminated from the objective by substitution of $I_t = \sum_{\tau=1}^{t} y_\tau - D_t$. Furthermore, constraints (4.2a) and (4.2b) assure that in each period t cumulative production is at least equal to cumulative demand. Moreover, constraints (4.3) are the coupling constraints between setup and production variables, and (4.4) are the integrality conditions on setup and production variables.

Throughout this section we make the following assumptions with respect to the input parameters :

Assumption 4.1

(a) setup cost (S_t), holding cost (h_t), and production cost (p_t) are unrestricted in sign.

(b) demand is binary $(d_t \in \{0,1\})$

(c) production rate equals one $(r = 1)$

(d) starting inventory is zero $(I_0 = 0)$

(e) ending inventory is zero $(I_T = 0)$

(f) initial machine state is idle $(y_0 = 0)$.

□

Additionally, the following definition will be useful in our discussion:

Definition: Analogous to Chapter 3, we define a deadline t_n as the n-th period in which demand equals one, and DL as the number of

deadlines. (Note that $DL = D_T$ by definition). Furthermore, for practical purposes we set $t_0 = 0$ and $t_{DL+1} = T + 1$. Finally, $\mathcal{D}$ is the ordered set of deadline periods, thus $\mathcal{D} = \{0\} \cup \{t \mid d_t = 1\} \cup \{T + 1\}$.
□

The LP relaxation of the integer program stated above can be strengthened by adding non-trivial *valid inequalities* to it. Until now we were able to derive one set of non-trivial valid inequalities, which will be called $(\tilde{t}_1, \tilde{t}_2, \tilde{t}_3)$-inequalities, since *three* planning periods are involved (note that these planning periods are not necessarily deadlines).

Lemma 4.1 ($(\tilde{t}_1, \tilde{t}_2, \tilde{t}_3)$-inequalities) *If,*

- $\tilde{t}_1 < \tilde{t}_2 < \tilde{t}_3$ *and,*

- $d_{\tilde{t}_1} = 0$ *and* $D_{\tilde{t}_2} = D_{\tilde{t}_1} + \tilde{t}_2 - \tilde{t}_1$ *and,*

- $D_{\tilde{t}_3} = D_{\tilde{t}_2} + 1$

then

$$\sum_{t=1}^{\tilde{t}_2} y_t + \sum_{t=\tilde{t}_1+1}^{\tilde{t}_3} v_t \geq D_{\tilde{t}_2} + 1 \tag{4.5}$$

is a valid inequality.

Proof: One of the following two complementary cases occurs:

    Case 1: $v_t = 1$ for some $t \in [\tilde{t}_1 + 1, \tilde{t}_3]$. In this case it is evident that (4.5) is a valid inequality.

    Case 2: $v_t = 0$ for all $t \in [\tilde{t}_1 + 1, \tilde{t}_3]$. Then production of $D_{\tilde{t}_3}$ must have taken place in the interval $[1, \tilde{t}_2]$. Since $D_{\tilde{t}_3} = D_{\tilde{t}_2} + 1$, it is clear that (4.5) is also a valid inequality in this case.

Consequently, $(\tilde{t}_1, \tilde{t}_2, \tilde{t}_3)$-inequalities are valid inequalities.
□

Remark: Although the $(\tilde{t}_1, \tilde{t}_2, \tilde{t}_3)$-inequalities may improve the lower bounds obtained by solving the LP relaxation of DLSP, they do not guarantee all-integer solutions for this relaxation.
Research, to find out whether $(\tilde{t}_1, \tilde{t}_2, \tilde{t}_3)$-inequalities are *facets* is still in progress.

Instead of solving the single-item DLSP by an algorithm based on the (strengthened) LP-relaxation of $1/1/TD/G/A$, in combination with a branch-and-bound procedure, problem $1/1/TD/G/A$ can also be solved by the following forward DP-algorithm:

$$C_t(0,0) = 0$$

and for $t = 1, .., T$,

$$C_t(n,k) = \begin{cases} \min(C_{t-1}(n,1), C_{t-1}(n,0)) & \text{if } k = 0 \\[2ex] \min(C_{t-1}(n-1,1), C_{t-1}(n-1,0)+S_t)+ \\ +h_{t,T}+p_t & \text{if } k = 1 \end{cases}$$

where $C_t(n,k)$ is the total minimal costs for periods 1 to t, when n units have been produced, and the machine status is k. Here, $k = 1$ represents a production period, whereas $k = 0$ represents an idle period. Note that in each period t, the condition $D_t \leq n \leq t$ must be satisfied for feasibility. Moreover, the minimal total costs are equal to $\min_k\{C_T(D_T, k)\} - \sum_{t=1}^{T} h_t D_t$. The reader may verify that the running-time of this DP-algorithm is $\mathcal{O}(TD_T)$.

4.3   A Strong LP-formulation

In this section we show that a solution for DLSP (under some additional assumptions on the input parameters), can be found by solving a linear programming model introduced below. This linear program will be called *Reformulated* DLSP (RDLSP). It is basically an *assignment problem*, with additional restrictions to account for setup costs.

RDLSP:

$$Z_{RDLSP} = \min \sum_{t \in \mathcal{D}} \sum_{s=1}^{t} \{S_s u_{s,t} + h_{s,t-1} z_{s,t}\} \tag{4.6}$$

subject to

$$\sum_{s=1}^{t} z_{s,t} = 1 \qquad\qquad t \in \mathcal{D} \tag{4.7}$$

$$\sum_{\substack{t \in \mathcal{D} \\ t \geq s}} z_{s,t} \leq 1 \qquad\qquad s = 1, \ldots, T \tag{4.8}$$

$$u_{s,t_n} \geq z_{s,t_n} - z_{s-1,t_{n-1}} \begin{cases} n = 2, \ldots, DL; \; s = 1, \ldots, t_n \\ t_{n-1} \geq s - 1 \geq 1 \end{cases} \tag{4.9}$$

$$u_{s,t_n} \geq z_{s,t_n} \begin{cases} n = 1, \ldots, DL; \; ; \; s = 1, \ldots, t_n \\ t_{n-1} < s - 1 \end{cases} \tag{4.10}$$

$$0 \leq u_{s,t} \leq 1 \qquad\qquad t \in \mathcal{D} \; ; \; s = 1, \ldots, t \tag{4.11}$$

$$z_{s,t} \geq 0 \qquad\qquad t \in \mathcal{D} \; ; \; s = 1, \ldots, t \tag{4.12}$$

In RDLSP the variable $z_{s,t}$ denotes the production quantity produced in period s to fulfil demand in period t ($\in \mathcal{D}$). The variable $u_{s,t}$ equals one if a setup takes place in period s and $z_{s,t} = 1$. The objective function is represented by (4.6) and the restrictions (4.7) and (4.8) assure that demand is fulfilled without backlogging and that capacity limitations are not violated, respectively. Restrictions (4.9) and (4.10) relate setup and production variables and restrictions (4.11) and (4.12) guarantee that setup and production variables are bounded by zero and one.

With respect to the problem parameters we make the following assumption:

Assumption 4.2

(a) *Setup costs (S_t) are non-negative and non-increasing in t.*

(b) *Holding costs (h_t) are non-negative.*

(c) *The sum of setup costs and inventory holding costs is positive in each period t, thus $S_t + h_t > 0$.*

□

Note that Assumption 4.2 (b) implies that $h_{\tilde{t}_1,\tilde{t}_2}$ is non-increasing in $\tilde{t}_1$ for fixed $\tilde{t}_2$.

In what follows, we use the concept of *production batches*, as defined below.

<u>**Definition:**</u> We define a production batch as an *uninterrupted* sequence of production periods, that can be constructed from any solution (z, u) of RDLSP in the following way:

Step 1: Take an arbitrary i for which $\min\{z_{s,t_i}, u_{s,t_i}\} > 0$. Let ℓ be equal to the smallest k (≥ 0) for which $z_{s+k,t_{i+k}}$ is equal to zero. If such k does not exist, put ℓ equal to $D_T + 1 - i$. Let j be equal to $i + \ell$.

Step 2: Compute the batch *amplitudes*, $\Delta_{s,i,j}$ through
$$\Delta_{s,i,j} = \min\{u_{s,t_i}, \min_{0 \leq k < \ell} z_{s+k,t_{i+k}}\}.$$

Step 3: Reduce the quantities u_{s,t_i} and $z_{s+k,t_{i+k}}$ $(k = 0, .., \ell - 1)$ by an amount $\Delta_{s,i,j}$.

□

The batch that we obtain in this manner starts in period s and fulfils (part of) the demand in the periods t_i until t_{j-1}. In what follows, we denote this batch by $\mathcal{B}_{s,i,j}$.

By executing steps 1, 2 and 3 iteratively until all $z_{s,t}$ are equal to zero, we ultimately obtain a complete split-up into batches of the solution of RDLSP. Note that, by doing so, inequalities (4.9) and (4.10) remain satisfied.

In addition to the concept of production batches, we introduce the network $\mathcal{N}$, of which the construction is explained in the definition below:

Definition: Let the network $\mathcal{N}$ consist of the set of nodes $i \ (= 1, \ldots, D_T + 1)$, corresponding to the deadlines, and the set of arcs from node i to node j, corresponding to the possible starting times s $(= 1, \ldots, t_i)$ of batch $\mathcal{B}_{s,i,j}$. In what follows, we denote an arc of $\mathcal{N}$, corresponding to the batch $\mathcal{B}_{s,i,j}$, by (s, i, j). Moreover, we associate with an arc (s, i, j) a cost of $S_s + \sum_{k=0}^{j-i-1} h_{s+k,t_{i+k}-1}$ per unit flow.
□

Lemma 4.2 *Any solution to RDLSP defines through the batch amplitudes Δ a flow of magnitude one in a network flow problem on $\mathcal{N}$.*

Proof: The following two assertions must be shown to hold:

Assertions:

(i)   *(outflow at node 1) = 1*

(ii) *(outflow at node $k + 1$) = (inflow at node $k + 1$) ($k \geq 1$).*

Assertion (i) holds since

$$(\text{outflow at node 1}) \quad = \quad \sum_{s,j} \Delta_{s,1,j}$$

$$= \quad (\text{total production for } t_1)$$

$$= \quad 1$$

Assertion *(ii)* holds since

$$1 \quad = \quad (\text{production for period } t_k)$$

$$= \quad \sum_{\substack{s,i,j \\ i \le k \le j-1}} \Delta_{s,i,j}$$

$$= \quad \sum_{\substack{s,i,j \\ i \le k < j-1}} \Delta_{s,i,j} + \sum_{s,i} \Delta_{s,i,k+1}$$

and

$$1 \quad = \quad (\text{production for period } t_{k+1})$$

$$= \quad \sum_{\substack{s,i,j \\ i \le k+1 < j}} \Delta_{s,i,j}$$

$$= \quad \sum_{\substack{s,i,j \\ i < k+1 < j}} \Delta_{s,i,j} + \sum_{s,j} \Delta_{s,k+1,j}$$

From this, it follows that

$$(\text{outflow at node } k+1) \quad = \quad \sum_{s,j} \Delta_{s,k+1,j}$$

$$= \quad \sum_{s,i} \Delta_{s,i,k+1}$$

$$= \quad (\text{inflow at node } k+1)$$

proving assertion *(ii)*

One readily verifies that a RDLSP solution (z, u) has a cost that equals the cost incurred by the unit flow on the network $\mathcal{N}$, given through a batch splitting of (z, u).
□

Next, we show that every extremal optimal solution to the network flow problem on $\mathcal{N}$ is feasible with respect to RDLSP. To do so, we state the following lemma:

Lemma 4.3 *Every extremal optimal flow Δ on the network creates non overlapping batches, that is, for any nonzero pair of flow variables $\Delta_{s,i,j}$, $\Delta_{t,m,n}$ with $i \leq m$ and $(s,i,j) \neq (t,m,n)$ it holds that*

$$s + j - i - 1 < t \ .$$

Proof: Assume, ad absurdum, that $s + j - i - 1 \geq t$ for two different nonzero batch amplitudes $\Delta_{s,i,j}$ and $\Delta_{t,m,n}$.

First, note for any pair of such overlapping batches that, if $i = m$, then, since $\Delta_{s,i,j} = 1 = \Delta_{t,m,n}$, node $i(= m)$ would have an outflow of magnitude 2. This is impossible and therefore $i < m$. Second, suppose that $t = t_m$. Then, as $s \leq t_i$, we would obtain

$$t_i + j - i - 1 \geq t_m \geq t_j$$

which is impossible. So $t < t_m$.

Next, define

$$\overline{m} = \min\{m' \in \{1, \ldots, D_T\} |\ \exists\, (s', i', j') \text{ and } (t', n') \text{ such that}$$
$$\Delta_{s',i',j'} = 1 = \Delta_{t',m',n'} \text{ with}$$
$$(s', i', j') \neq (t', m', n') \text{ and}$$
$$i' \leq m' \text{ and } s' + j' - i' - 1 \geq t'\}.$$

Informally $\overline{m}$ is the first period number for which untimely production starts, in the sense, that production for $\overline{m}$ overlaps with, or precedes production for previous demand periods.

Let $\Delta_{\overline{s},\overline{i},\overline{j}}$ and $\Delta_{\overline{t},\overline{m},\overline{n}}$ give rise to overlapping batches, and consider the nonzero batch amplitude $\Delta_{\tilde{s},\tilde{m},\overline{m}}$ that enters node $\overline{m}$. We have $\overline{i} < \overline{m}$ and $\overline{t} < t_{\overline{m}}$.

Also either,

1. $\overline{i} = \tilde{m}$ and so $(\overline{s}, \overline{i}, \overline{j}) = (\tilde{s}, \tilde{m}, \overline{m})$ and thus $\Delta_{\tilde{s},\tilde{m},\overline{m}}$ overlaps with $\Delta_{\overline{t},\overline{m},\overline{n}}$, or

2. $\tilde{\imath} < \tilde{m} < \overline{m}$ and so, by the definition of $\overline{m}$, $\Delta_{\overline{s},\overline{\imath},\overline{\jmath}}$ does not overlap with $\Delta_{\tilde{s},\tilde{m},\overline{m}}$.

In the first case $\tilde{s} + \overline{m} - \tilde{m} - 1 \geq \overline{\imath}$. In the second case, $\overline{s} + \overline{\jmath} - \overline{\imath} - 1 < \tilde{s}$ and it follows, using $\overline{s} + \overline{\jmath} - \overline{\imath} - 1 \geq \overline{\imath}$, that $\overline{\imath} \leq \tilde{s} + \overline{m} - \tilde{m} - 1$ again. But $\overline{\imath} \leq \tilde{s} + \overline{m} - \tilde{m} - 1$ implies that the batches with amplitudes $\Delta_{\tilde{s},\tilde{m},\overline{m}}$ and $\Delta_{\overline{\imath},\overline{m},\overline{n}}$ can be transformed into a single batch starting in $\tilde{s}$ by delaying the batch with amplitude $\Delta_{\overline{\imath},\overline{m},\overline{n}}$ over $\tilde{s} + \overline{m} - \tilde{m} - \overline{\imath} \, (\geq 1)$ periods. This results in a cost difference given as:

$$S_{\overline{\imath}} + \sum_{k=0}^{\overline{m}-\overline{n}-1} h_{\overline{\imath}+k, t_{\overline{m}+k}-1} - \sum_{k=0}^{\overline{m}-\overline{n}-1} h_{\tilde{s}+\overline{m}-\tilde{m}+k, t_{\overline{m}+k}-1} > 0$$

which is implied by Assumption 4.2. Thus a contradiction arises with the fact that Δ is optimal. Therefore we conclude that under Assumption 4.2 overlapping batches are not created by optimal flows, and consequently, at most one unit is produced per period.
□

Remark: It can be seen easily that there exists an optimal flow Δ in the network $\mathcal{N}$, for which every nonzero flow $\Delta_{s,i,j}$ uses the least cost arc $s = t_i$.

Based on the above lemmas, integrality of RDLSP is stated below:

Theorem 4.1 *Under Assumption 4.2 every optimal extremal solution to RDLSP is all-integer*

Proof: Upto now we have shown that every solution to RDLSP can be transformed (under equal costs) into a unit flow Δ on the network $\mathcal{N}$ (Lemma 4.2). Moreover, every extremal optimal solution to the minimum cost flow problem on $\mathcal{N}$ is feasible with respect to RDLSP (Lemma 4.3). It remains to be shown that every extremal optimal solution (z, u) to RDLSP results in an extremal flow Δ after batch splitting, for then (z, u) is integer too. To prove extremality of Δ, take (z, u) extremal and optimal for RDLSP and do batch splitting to obtain the unit flows Δ.

Suppose, ad absurdum, that Δ is not extremal and therefore, is a convex, nontrivial, combination of two other, necessarily also optimal, flows. As a consequence of Lemma 4.3 these flows can be used to construct the production quantities for two different solutions to RDLSP with minimum cost that combine exactly as the flows convexly to form the solution (z, u). But this is impossible as (z, u) is extremal. So we conclude that Δ is extremal. Hence Δ is binary. Therefore also (z, u) is binary.

This completes the proof that all extremal optimal solutions to RDLSP are all-integer under Assumption 4.2.

□

The optimal solution obtained for RDLSP in terms of (z, u) variables, can easily be transformed into an optimal solution in terms of (y, v) variables of DLSP, and vice versa. Therefore, consider the map $\mathcal{M}$ from the set of RDLSP solutions to the set of DLSP solutions given by $y_s = \sum_t z_{s,t}$ and $v_s = \min\{1, \sum_t u_{s,t}\}$.

Corollary 4.1 *Under the map $\mathcal{M}$ an optimal solution of RDLSP is mapped onto an optimal solution of DLSP and every optimal solution of DLSP is the image under $\mathcal{M}$ of an optimal solution of RDLSP.*

Proof: The only non-evident assertion is that every optimal solution of DLSP is the image under $\mathcal{M}$ of an optimal solution of RDLSP. However this follows readily by observing that an optimal (y, v) solution can be transformed into an optimal (z, u) solution, using the following transformation for the z variables:

$$
z_{s,t} = \begin{cases} 1 & \text{if } s = s_k \text{ and } t = t_k \\ 0 & \text{otherwise.} \end{cases}
$$

where $s_k = \min\{s \mid \sum_{\tau=1}^{s} y_\tau = k\}$.

The variables $u_{s,t}$ can be obtained in a similar way. For the constructed solution (z, u) one easily verifies that application of $\mathcal{M}$ yields (y, v).

□

Remark: The example below shows that an instance of RDLSP, not satisfying Assumption 4.2, can be constructed, for which the extremal optimal solution is fractional.

Example:

Consider the following problem data:

t	1	2	3
d_t	0	1	1
S_t	1	1	5
p_t	1	4	0

where p_t are the production costs for period t. The optimal (z, u) solution to this problem is given by: $z_{1,2} = \frac{1}{2}$, $z_{1,3} = \frac{1}{2}$, $z_{2,2} = \frac{1}{2}$, $z_{3,3} = \frac{1}{2}$, $u_{1,2} = \frac{1}{2}$, $u_{1,3} = \frac{1}{2}$, $u_{2,2} = \frac{1}{2}$, while all other variables are zero. The value of the objective $Z_{RDLSP} = 4\frac{1}{2}$.

4.4   A Dynamic Programming approach

In this section we formulate a Dynamic Programming (DP) algorithm for single item DLSP problems, satisfying Assumption 4.2. The algorithm is inspired by the $\mathcal{O}(T \log T)$ algorithm for the Wagner-Whitin problem, due to Wagelmans, Van Hoesel and Kolen [106]. Before we present a detailed description of our DP algorithm, we state in the following theorem an important structure-property of DLSP:

Theorem 4.2 (Zero-Switch property) *Under Assumption 4.2, there exists an optimal solution (y, v) to DLSP, such that:*

$$v_t(I_{t-1} + (1 - d_t)) = 0 .$$

Proof: This theorem follows as an immediate consequence of the remark made after Lemma 4.3 (Section 4.3).
□

Definition: Let $C(t)$ $(t \in \mathcal{D})$ be the minimal total cost to fulfil demand in periods t until T (under the assumption of zero inventory at the start of period t).
□

The Zero-Switch property enables us to find an optimal solution to DLSP by using the following backward DP recursion:

$$C(t_{DL+1}) = 0$$

$$C(t_n) = \min_{t \in \mathcal{F}_n} \{S_{t_n} + H(t_n, t) + C(t)\} \quad \text{for } n = DL, .., 1. \quad (4.13)$$

where

$$H(t_n, t) = \sum_{k=0}^{D_t - D_{t_n} - 1} h_{t_n + k, T}$$

and $\mathcal{F}_n \equiv \{t_k, t_{k+1}, \ldots, t_{DL+1}\}$, with k such that

$$k = \min\{j > n \mid d_{t_j - 1} = 0 \text{ and } d_{t_j} = 1\}.$$

In the following we will establish how this DP can be streamlined to become very efficient. The streamlining is implemented through replacement at each stage n in the DP of $\mathcal{F}_n$ by an *ordered* set $\mathcal{L}_n \subset \{t_{n+1}, \ldots, t_{DL+1}\}$, such that the minimum in (4.13) occurs for the last element in $\mathcal{L}_n$. The key to the efficiency of the streamlined DP, as we will show, is that $\mathcal{L}_{n-1} \subset \{t_n\} \cup \mathcal{L}_n$ and that the *ordered* set $\mathcal{L}_{n-1}$ can be constructed fast from the ordered set $\mathcal{L}_n$ (and some extra information).

In the explanation of our algorithm, the concept of *dominance*, as defined below, plays an important role.

Definition: For $t, t' \geq \tau$, we say that $t \in \mathcal{D} \setminus \{0\}$ *dominates* $t' \in \mathcal{D} \setminus \{0\}$ *with respect to* $\tau \in \mathcal{D} \setminus \{0\}$, if

$$S_\tau + H(\tau, t) + C(t) \leq S_\tau + H(\tau, t') + C(t')$$

or equivalently,

$$C(t) - C(t') \leq H(\tau, t') - H(\tau, t) .$$

In what follows, we denote dominance of t over t' with respect to τ by $t \xrightarrow{\tau} t'$, or by $t' \xleftarrow{\tau} t$.

□

As a result of the special cost structure of DLSP, we are able to derive a structure-property with respect to the holding costs, which turns out to be crucial for our algorithm.

Theorem 4.3 (Holding Cost Property) *Under Assumption 4.2 it holds that for $m_1 < m_2$ the difference $H(t_n, t_{m_2}) - H(t_n, t_{m_1})$ is nonincreasing in n, for $n = 1, .., m_1 - 1$.*

Proof: After simple calculations we obtain that

$$H(t_n, t_{m_2}) - H(t_n, t_{m_1}) - [H(t_{n+1}, t_{m_2}) - H(t_{n+1}, t_{m_1})] =$$

$$\sum_{k=0}^{D_{t_{m_2}} - D_{t_{m_1}}} (h_{t_n + D_{t_{m_1}} - D_{t_n} + k, T} - h_{t_{n+1} + D_{t_{m_1}} - D_{t_{n+1}} + k, T}) .$$

Since $h_{t,T}$ is nonincreasing in t, it is sufficient to show that $t_n + D_{t_{m_1}} - D_{t_n} \leq t_{n+1} + D_{t_{m_1}} - D_{t_{n+1}}$. But this is obvious, because demand is binary so that $D_{t_{n+1}} - D_{t_n} \leq t_{n+1} - t_n$.

□

As a direct consequence of this structure-property, the following two corollary's hold:

Corollary 4.2 *For $t_{m_1}, t_{m_2} \in \mathcal{F}_n$ with $t_{m_1} < t_{m_2}$ it holds that if $t_{m_1} \xrightarrow{t_n} t_{m_2}$, then $t_{m_1} \xrightarrow{t} t_{m_2}$ for $t_n > t \in \mathcal{D}$.*

Corollary 4.3 *For each pair of periods $t_{m_1}, t_{m_2} \in \mathcal{D} \setminus \{0\}$, with $t_{m_1} < t_{m_2}$, there exists a "reversal" period $r(t_{m_1}, t_{m_2}) \in \mathcal{D}$ with $r(t_{m_1}, t_{m_2}) \leq t_{m_1}$ such that the following condition holds*

$$(t_{m_1} \geq t \text{ and } t_{m_1} \xrightarrow{t} t_{m_2}) \iff r(t_{m_1}, t_{m_2}) \geq t$$

for $t \in \mathcal{D} \setminus \{0\}$.

Having introduced dominance, and two important structure properties, we now turn to introducing the sets $\mathcal{L}_n$.

Definition:. For $1 \leq n \leq DL + 1$ the set $\tilde{\mathcal{L}}_n \equiv \{\tau_i^n\}_{i=1}^{|\tilde{\mathcal{L}}_n|}$ is defined as the largest ordered subset of $\{t_{n+1}, \ldots, t_{DL+1}\}$ such that,

$$t \in \tilde{\mathcal{L}}_n \Rightarrow \not\exists s \in \mathcal{D}: \ t_{n+1} \leq s < t \text{ such that } s \xrightarrow{t_n} t .$$

We now define $\mathcal{L}_n \equiv \{t_i^n\}_{i=1}^{|\mathcal{L}_n|}$ as the maximal (ordered) subset of $\tilde{\mathcal{L}}_n$ such that,

$$t_j \in \mathcal{L}_n \Longrightarrow \not\exists t_i, t_k \in \tilde{\mathcal{L}}_n \text{ with } t_i < t_j < t_k \text{ and } r(t_i, t_j) \geq r(t_j, t_k) .$$

Note that the set $\mathcal{L}_n$ has the following structure:

1) $t_{n+1} = t_1^n < \ldots < t_{|\mathcal{L}_n|}^n$,

2) $t_{n+1} = t_1^n \xleftarrow{t_n} \ldots \xleftarrow{t_n} t_{|\mathcal{L}_n|}^n$,

3) $r(t_i^n, t_{i+1}^n) < r(t_{i+1}^n, r_{i+2}^n) \quad$ for $i = 1, \ldots, |\mathcal{L}_n| - 2$.

□

During the DP algorithm we will construct the sequence of subsets $\mathcal{L}_{DL+1}, \mathcal{L}_{DL}, \mathcal{L}_{DL-1}, \ldots, \mathcal{L}_1$ by recursion. First we have to establish that the recursion given as,

$$C(t_{DL+1}) = 0$$
$$C(t_n) = S_{t_n} + H(t_n, t_{|\mathcal{L}_n|}^n) + C(t_{|\mathcal{L}_n|}^n) \quad \text{for } n = DL, \ldots, 1.$$

is valid. For validity to hold it is sufficient to prove the following lemma.

Lemma 4.4 *For each n it holds*

$$H(t_n, t_{|\mathcal{L}_n|}^n) + C(t_{|\mathcal{L}_n|}^n) \leq H(t_n, t_\ell) + C(t_\ell)$$

for all $\ell = n + 1, \ldots, DL + 1$.

Proof: Let t^* be the smallest period t (strictly) larger than t_n for which

$$H(t_n, t) + C(t)$$

is minimal. Then, obviously $t^* \in \tilde{\mathcal{L}}_n$. So, $\tau^n_{|\tilde{\mathcal{L}}_n|} \xrightarrow{t_n} t^*$. But since t^* is a "minimizing period" it dominates all other periods in $\{t_{n+1}, \ldots, t_{DL+1}\}$ and thus a fortiori $\tau^n_{|\tilde{\mathcal{L}}_n|}$. Therefore

$$H(t_n, t^*) + C(t^*) = H(t_n, \tau^n_{|\tilde{\mathcal{L}}_n|}) + C(\tau^n_{|\tilde{\mathcal{L}}_n|}) .$$

Noting that $\tau^n_{|\tilde{\mathcal{L}}_n|} = t^n_{|\mathcal{L}_n|}$ completes the proof of the lemma.
□

We now show how $\mathcal{L}_n$ can be obtained from $\mathcal{L}_{n+1}$. In particular, suppose we have the following data (for stage $n+1$)

Data known for stage $n+1$

- the ordered set $\mathcal{L}_{n+1}$,

- $r(t^{n+1}_i, t^{n+1}_{i+1})$ for $i = 1, \ldots, |\mathcal{L}_{n+1}| - 1$,

- $C(t_\ell)$ for $\ell = n+2, \ldots, DL+1$.

Then, the data for stage n can be computed using the following algorithm:

Algorithm for stage n:

Step 1 $C(t_{n+1}) = S_{t_{n+1}} + H(t_{n+1}, t^{n+1}_{|\mathcal{L}_{n+1}|}) + C(t^{n+1}_{|\mathcal{L}_{n+1}|})$,

Step 2 $\mathcal{L}'_n := \mathcal{L}_{n+1}$,

Step 3 if $r(t^{n+1}_{|\mathcal{L}_{n+1}|-1}, t^{n+1}_{|\mathcal{L}_{n+1}|}) = t_n$ then delete $t^{n+1}_{|\mathcal{L}_{n+1}|}$ from $\mathcal{L}'_n$,

Step 4 $\mathcal{L}'_n := \{t_{n+1}\} \bigcup \mathcal{L}'_n$,

Step 5 determine i^* as the largest i for which $t_{n+1} \xrightarrow{t_n} t^{n+1}_i$.
$\mathcal{L}'_n := \mathcal{L}'_n \setminus \bigcup_{i=1,\ldots,i^*} \{t^{n+1}_i\}$

Step 6 renumber $\mathcal{L}'_n$ and put $\mathcal{L}'_n \equiv \{t'_1, \ldots, t'_{|\mathcal{L}'_n|}\}$,

Step 7 compute i^* as the largest i for which $r(t'_1, t'_i) \geq r(t'_i, t'_{i+1})$.

$\mathcal{L}'_n := \mathcal{L}'_n \setminus \bigcup_{i=2,\ldots,i^*} \{t^{n+1}_i\}$;

note that the reversal periods are computed efficiently using *binary search*.

Step 8 renumber $\mathcal{L}'_n$.

The following lemma is easily verified and a formal proof is left to the reader.

Lemma 4.5 $\mathcal{L}_n = \mathcal{L}'_n$

Note that indeed by this lemma the computation preceding it shows how to compute the data for stage n from the data for stage $n+1$.

Before we assert the complexity of our streamlined DP-algorithm, we first explain how to compute $H(t_n, t_m)$ for arbitrary n and m in constant time. To do so, we need to perform the following preprocessing step:

Preprocessing Step: First, compute $h_{t,T}$ for all $t = 1, .., T$. Since $h_{t,T} = h_t + h_{t+1,T}$, this can be done in $\mathcal{O}(T)$. Secondly, compute $\sum_{\tau=t}^{T} h_{\tau,T}$ for $t = 1, .., T$. This can also be done by backward recursion in $\mathcal{O}(T)$.

Since $H(t_n, t_m) = \sum_{\tau=t_n}^{T} h_{\tau,T} - \sum_{\tau=t_n+D_{t_m}-D_{t_n}}^{T} h_{\tau,T}$, it is clear that computation can be performed in constant time.

Theorem 4.4 *The complexity of the streamlined DP-algorithm is* $\mathcal{O}(T + |\mathcal{D}| \log |\mathcal{D}|)$

Proof: We make the following observations:

(a) Preprocessing requires $\mathcal{O}(T)$.

(b) Step 1, Step 2, Step 3, Step 4, Step 6 and Step 8 require constant time and must be executed $|\mathcal{D}|$ times.

(c) At stage n Step 5 has a running time of $\mathcal{O}(f_n + 1)$, where f_n is the number of deletions performed during the computations at stage n. Since $\sum_n f_n \leq |\mathcal{D}|$, this step requires in total a running time of $\mathcal{O}(|\mathcal{D}|)$.

(d) Step 7 for stage n has a running time of $\mathcal{O}(f'_n \log |\mathcal{D}|)$, where f'_n is the number of deletions. Since $\sum_n f'_n \leq |\mathcal{D}|$, the overall running time of this step is $\mathcal{O}(|\mathcal{D}| \log |\mathcal{D}|)$.

From the four observations made above, it follows that the running time of the DP-based algorithm is $\mathcal{O}(T + |\mathcal{D}| \log |\mathcal{D}|)$.
$\square$

The streamlined DP algorithm is demonstrated by the following example:

Example: Consider the following six period $(T = 6)$ DLSP:

t	1	2	3	4	5	6
d_t	1	0	1	0	1	1
S_t	8	6	6	3	3	1
h_t	1	9	2	0	1	1

First, the cumulative holding costs $H(t_m, t_n)$ are computed:

	t_1	t_2	t_3	t_4	t_5
t_1	-	14	27	31	33
t_2	-	-	4	6	8
t_3	-	-	-	2	3
t_4	-	-	-	-	1

The algorithm proceeds now as follows:

Initialisation: $C(t_5) = 0$ and $\mathcal{L}_4 = \{t_5\}$

Stage n = 3

Step 1: $C(t_4) = S_{t_4} + H(t_4, t_5) + C(t_5) = 4$

Step 2: $\mathcal{L}_3' = \mathcal{L}_4 = \{t_5\}$

Step 4: $\mathcal{L}_3' = \{t_4\} \cup \mathcal{L}_3 = \{t_4, t_5\}$

Step 5: $r(t_4, t_5) = \min(\tau | C(t_4) - C(t_5) \leq H(\tau, t_5) - H(\tau, t_4))$. Such τ does however not exist.

Stage n = 2

Step 1: $C(t_3) = S_{t_3} + H(t_3, t_5) + C(t_5) = 6$

Step 2: $\mathcal{L}_2' = \mathcal{L}_3 = \{t_4, t_5\}$

Step 3:   Since $r(t_4, t_5)$ does not exist, $\mathcal{L}_2'$ is left unchanged.

Step 4: $\mathcal{L}_2' = \{t_4, t_5\} \cup \mathcal{L}_3 = \{t_3, t_4, t_5\}$

Step 5: $r(t_3, t_4) = t_2$ and $r(t_3, t_5) = t_1$. Thus, $i^* = 1$ and $\mathcal{L}_2' = \mathcal{L}_2' \setminus \{t_4\} = \{t_3, t_5\}$.

Stage n = 1

Step 1: $C(t_2) = S_{t_2} + H(t_2, t_5) + C(t_5) = 14$

Step 2: $\mathcal{L}_1' = \mathcal{L}_2 = \{t_3, t_5\}$

Step 3:   Since $r(t_3, t_5) = t_1$, $\mathcal{L}'_1 = \mathcal{L}'_1 \setminus \{t_5\} = \{t_3\}$

Step 4: $\mathcal{L}'_1 = \{t_2, t_3\}$

Step 5: $r(t_2, t_3) = t_1$. Thus, $i^* = 1$ and $\mathcal{L}'_1 = \mathcal{L}'_1 \setminus \{t_3\} = \{t_2\}$.

Stage n = 0

Step 1: $C(t_1) = S_{t_1} + H(t_1, t_2) + C(t_2) = 36$

Thus, total minimal costs are $C(t_1) - \sum_{t=1}^{T} h_t D_t = 15$ and setups are made in periods t_1 and t_2.

□

In case that setup costs and holding costs are non negative period independent constants, the running time of our DP-algorithm can be reduced, to $\mathcal{O}(T + |\mathcal{D}_0| \log |\mathcal{D}_0|)$, where $\mathcal{D}_0 = \{t \mid d_t = 1 \text{ and } d_{t-1} = 0\}$. This result is based on a structure-property, as stated in the following lemma:

Lemma 4.6 *If setup costs and holding costs are non negative period independent constants, there exists an optimal solution for which setups will only take place in periods $t \in \mathcal{D}_0$.*

The proof of this lemma is based on simple production shifting arguments and is left to the reader.

4.5   Summary and discussion

In this chapter the single item Discrete Lotsizing and Scheduling (DLSP) problem is considered. A set of explicit valid inequalities is derived, which can be added to the LP relaxation of DLSP, to obtain stronger lower bounds in an enumeration type of algorithm to solve the problem. In addition, we present a straightforward DP-algorithm, with a running time of $\mathcal{O}(TD_T)$. It is further proved that an alternative IP formulation

for DLSP exists (based on the plant location problem and variable splitting for production *and* setup variables), for which the LP-relaxation,
solved by the simplex-method, yields all-integer solutions under certain
restrictions on the input parameters. Disadvantage of this formulation
is that it does not use the original (y, v) variables in which DLSP is
defined, but instead (z, u) variables, so a complete explicit description
of the (integer) convex hull of DLSP in the original variables is still an
open problem. Finally, a DP-algorithm is presented which uses special
properties of optimal DLSP solutions and requires $\mathcal{O}(T + |\mathcal{D}| \log |\mathcal{D}|)$
computation time (again, under special assumptions with respect to
the cost parameters). If setup costs and holding costs are time inde-
pendent, the running time can even be reduced to $\mathcal{O}(T + |\mathcal{D}_0| \log |\mathcal{D}_0|)$.

As already mentioned in the introduction of this chapter, the methods
for solving single-item problems as presented here are important when
developing (decomposition) algorithms and cutting plane algorithms
for solving *multi-item* problems. In these algorithms single item problems occur as subproblems, when relaxing capacity constraints. For a
successful implementation of such decomposition methods, it is essential that the single item problems can be solved very fast, as we will
see in Chapter 5, which deals with multi-item problems.

Chapter 5

The Multi-item DLSP

5.1 Introduction

In this chapter we consider algorithms for solving the multi-item DLSP. In Section 5.2 solution procedures are discussed, based on straightforward application of dynamic programming. Although these algorithms give exact solutions, the computation times and the required memory grow rapidly with the size of the problem. Therefore, alternative (approximation) algorithms are considered, that give acceptable solutions in reasonable computation time for problem dimensions as met in practice. Section 5.3 presents the algorithms as proposed by Fleischmann for solving multi-item, single facility problems with zero setup times ($1/N/SI/G/A$ and $1/N/SD/G/A$). These algorithms are based on Lagrangean relaxation and dynamic programming to obtain lower bounds, while successive approximation techniques are used to obtain upper bounds. The procedures are embedded in a branch-and-bound routine. In Section 5.4 two heuristics are described for the multi-item single facility DLSP with nonzero setup times ($1/N/SI/G/SI$). The heuristics are based on column generation techniques. In both heuristics new columns are generated using DP, but the heuristics differ in the way the *master problem* is solved. The *primal* heuristic uses standard linear programming, while the *dual* heuristic uses a dual ascent procedure combined with subgradient optimization. In addition, both heuristics contain procedures to search for feasible solutions.

Section 5.5 reports on a computational comparison between the heuristics and Section 5.6 presents a brief summary and a discussion of the results.

5.2   Dynamic Programming algorithms

To illustrate the DP-approach for solving multi-item DLSP problems, we present an algorithm for solving $1/N/SI/G/A$, formulated in Chapter 2. The algorithm uses a cost function $C_t(n_1, .., n_i, .., n_N, k)$, which is the minimal total cost up to period t, assuming n_i periods of production for item i. If the machine produces in period t, the state variable k denotes the item number for which it produces, while $k = 0$ when the machine is idle in period t.

Assuming that the initial machine state is idle, the forward recursion reads:

$$C_0(0, .., 0, .., 0, 0) = 0$$

and for $t = 1, .., T$

$$C_t(n_1, .., n_i, .., n_N, k) = \begin{cases} \min_{k'}[C_{t-1}(n_1', .., n_i', .., n_N', k') + \\ + S_k(1 - \varphi_k(k'))] + p_{k,t} + H_t & \text{if } k \neq 0 \\ \\ \min_{k'}[C_{t-1}(n_1', .., n_i', .., n_N', k')] + \\ + H_t & \text{if } k = 0 \end{cases}$$

where $\varphi_i(k) = 1$ if $i = k$, and $\varphi_i(k) = 0$ otherwise.
Furthermore, $H_t = \sum_{i=1}^{N} h_i(n_i - D_{i,t})$, and $n_i' = n_i - \varphi_i(k)$. Note that, due to feasibility requirements, the cost function in period t is only defined when n_i satisfies $D_{i,t} \leq n_i \leq \min(t - \sum_{j \neq i} D_{j,t}, D_{i,T})$, and when the cost function $C_{t-1}(n_1', .., n_i', .., n_N', k')$ is defined for some k'.
The costs of an optimal production schedule are given by $\min_k[C_T(D_{1,T}, .., D_{i,T}, .., D_{N,T}, k)]$, and the running time of the algorithm is $\mathcal{O}(N^2 T \Pi_{i=1}^{N} D_{i,T})$.
The proposed DP algorithm can easily be extended to handle several

other variants of DLSP, covered by our six-field notation (see [94]). However, although these DP algorithms run in polynomial time when both the number of items (N) and the number of machines (M) are part of the problem description, computation times and memory requirements will become prohibitively large for all but very small problem instances. As a result, these DP algorithms are mainly of theoretical interest. For this reason we must resort to alternative algorithms, as will be discussed in the remainder of this chapter.

5.3 Problems with zero setup time

In this section we discuss an algorithm due to Fleischmann [40] for the multi-item, single machine problem with sequence-independent setup costs ($1/N/SI/G/A$). Moreover, we consider an extension of this algorithm (see also [41]), to problems with sequence-dependent setup costs ($1/N/SD/G/A$).

5.3.1 Fleischmann's algorithm for 1/N/SI/G/A

For the readers convenience we repeat the mathematical model formulation from Chapter 3 for the multi-item, single machine problem with sequence-independent setup-costs:

$1/N/SI/G/A$:

$$Z_{DLSP} = \min \sum_{i=1}^{N} \sum_{t=1}^{T} (S_i v_{i,t} + c_{i,t} y_{i,t}) - \sum_{i=1}^{N} \tilde{C}_i \qquad (5.1)$$

subject to

$$\sum_{\tau=1}^{t} y_{i,\tau} \geq D_{i,t} \qquad i = 1, .., N; \, t = 1, .., T-1 \qquad (5.2a)$$

$$\sum_{\tau=1}^{T} y_{i,\tau} = D_{i,T} \qquad i = 1, .., N \qquad (5.2b)$$

$$\sum_{i=1}^{N} y_{i,t} \leq 1 \qquad\qquad t = 1, .., T. \qquad (5.3)$$

$$v_{i,t} \geq y_{i,t} - y_{i,t-1} \qquad\qquad i = 1, .., N;\ t = 1, .., T \quad (5.4)$$

$$y_{i,t}, v_{i,t} \in \{0, 1\} \qquad\qquad i = 1, .., N;\ t = 1, .., T \quad (5.5)$$

where constants $c_{i,t} = h_i r_i (T - t + 1) + p_{i,t}$ and constants $\tilde{C}_i = \sum_{t=1}^{T} h_i (T - t + 1) d_{i,t} - T h_i I_{i,0}$. For an explanation of other variables, constants, the objective function (5.1) and constraint sets (5.2) to (5.5), the reader is referred to Chapter 3.

The algorithm for solving this problem consists of the following three subroutines:

- *A lower bounding procedure,*

- *An upper bounding heuristic,*

- *A branching strategy.*

Lower bounding procedure.

Lower bounds to problem $1/N/SI/G/A$ are computed by relaxing the capacity constraints (5.3), using non-positive Lagrange multipliers $u = (u_1, .., u_T)$. The Lagrangean problem decomposes into N single item problems $(LR(DLSP)_i)$ $(i = 1, .., N)$ which can be formulated as:

$LR(DLSP)_i$

$$Z_{LR(DLSP)_i}(u) = \min \sum_{t=1}^{T} (S_i v_{i,t} + (c_{i,t} - u_{i,t}) y_{i,t}) \qquad (5.6)$$

subject to

(5.2a), (5.2b), (5.4), (5.5)

The lower bounds obtained by solving $LR(DLSP)_i$ can even be improved by replacing the demand constraints (5.2) by the following set of constraints:

$$C_{i,t} \leq \sum_{\tau=1}^{t} y_{i,\tau} \leq t - \sum_{j \neq i} C_{j,t} \qquad \text{for } t = 1, .., T \quad (5.2')$$

where the constants $C_{i,t}$ are computed recursively as:

$$C_{i,T} = D_{i,T}$$

and for $t = T - 1, .., 1$

$$C_{i,t} = \max(C_{i,t+1} - 1, D_{i,t})$$

(Note that for feasibility of the overall problem it suffices to check whether $\sum_{i=1}^{N} C_{i,t} \leq t$ holds for each period t.) Lower bounds can now be computed by solving the Lagrangean problems $LR(DLSP)_i$, using a simple forward recursion with a time requirement of $\mathcal{O}(D_{i,T}T)$. New Lagrange multipliers u are computed using a *subgradient optimization technique*, which is described in Section 5.4.

Upper bounding heuristic.

Fleischmann proposes an upper bounding heuristic which is based on sequentially solving a modified version of the Lagrangean subproblems $LR(DLSP)_i$, thereby using the same Lagrange multipliers u as computed during the lower bounding procedure. To demonstrate this procedure in more detail, suppose we have generated production plans for items $1, .., i - 1$. When determining production for item i in period t, it suffices to check whether period t is not used for production by any other item $1, .., i - 1$ *and* the feasibility rule $\sum_{\tau=1}^{t} y_{i,\tau} \leq t - \sum_{j \neq i} C_{j,t}$ is not violated.

These constraints are added to the DP formulation as used for the lower bounding procedure and do not influence time requirements. Proceeding in this way for items $i + 1, .., N$ ultimately leads to a feasible multi-item solution (upper bound).

Branching strategy.

The branching strategy simply consists of fixing the production of a certain item in a certain period (thus, fixing variables $y_{i,t}$), starting with the last period and proceeding backwards to the first period. There is a simple criterion for checking the feasibility of the arising (sub)problems. To explain this criterion, suppose that for item i a production schedule is constructed for periods $t^* + 1, .., T$. The predetermined production variables are given by $\overline{y}_{i,t^*+1}, .., \overline{y}_{i,T}$. If we update the constants C_{i,t^*} as:

$$C_{i,t^*} = D_{i,T} - \sum_{\tau=t^*+1}^{T} \overline{y}_{i,\tau}$$

the remaining (sub)problem is feasible if and only if

$$\sum_{i=1}^{N} C_{i,t^*} \le t^*$$

This feasibility criterion is used in the branching procedure in such a way that backtracking due to infeasibility is no longer needed. The branching process is further speeded up by storing the production schedules that have already been evaluated in order to avoid duplicate calculations.

Fleischmann tested his procedure on a set of problems based on transformations of capacitated lot sizing problems (CLSP) as stated in Thizy and Van Wassenhove [100], Dixon and Silver [30] and Günther [54]. The results were encouraging and Fleischmann concluded that *"DLSP can be used for modelling capacitated multi-product dynamic lot-sizing problems in more detail than the CLSP and at once provides computational advantages "*. Other test results for this algorithm on a set of randomly generated DLSP problems are found in Section 5.5.

5.3.2   Fleischmann's algorithm for 1/N/SD/G/A

The multi-item, single machine problem with sequence-dependent setup costs, general production costs, and zero setup times is mathematically formulated as:

$1/N/SD/G/A$:

$$Z_{DLSP} = \min \sum_{i=1}^{N} \sum_{t=1}^{T} \left(\sum_{j=1}^{N} S_{j,i} \max(0, y_{i,t} + y_{j,t-1} - 1) + c_{i,t} y_{i,t} \right) \quad (5.7)$$

subject to

$(5.2')$, (5.3), (5.5)

The algorithm for solving this problem is based on the algorithm for the problem with sequence-independent setup costs as presented in Section 5.3.1. To obtain *lower bounds*, the capacity constraints (5.3) are relaxed using non-positive Lagrange multipliers u. Contrary to the problem with sequence-independent setup costs, this relaxation does not decompose the problem directly into N single item problems, since setup costs still link the subproblems. If sequence-dependent setup costs are replaced by (approximation of) sequence- independent setup costs, the problem indeed decomposes into single item problems $LR(DLSP)_i$. Here, the following *approximation* of sequence-independent setup costs $\widehat{S}_i$ is suggested:

$$\widehat{S}_i = S_i^{(1)} + S_i^{(2)}$$

where $S_i^{(1)} = \min_{k \neq i} S_{k,i}$ and $S_i^{(2)} = \min_{k \neq i}(S_{i,k} - S_k^{(1)})$. Note that total setup costs are *underestimated* since $S_{i,j} \geq S_j^{(1)} + S_i^{(2)}$. Consequently, the solution obtained by solving the single item problems forms a *true* lower bound.

Upper bounds are obtained by sequentially solving the same single item problems that appear in the lower bounding procedure, thereby *blocking* periods already used for other items. In addition, the under estimation of setup costs has to be corrected in the cost function: If production for item i takes place in period t, the costs for items $j = i+1, .., N$ in periods $t-1$ and $t+1$ are updated as $c_{j,t-1} = c_{j,t-1} + S_{j,i} - S_i^{(1)} - S_j^{(2)}$

and $c_{j,t+1} = c_{j,t+1} + S_{i,j} - S_j^{(1)} - S_i^{(2)}$.

The *branching strategy* implemented by Fleischmann and Popp is exactly the same as proposed for $1/N/SI/G/A$. The procedure has been tested on a limited number of real life problems. The results are however not very encouraging (the gap between lower and upper bound goes up to 50 %), which is caused by the poor quality of lower bounds obtained by the suggested lower bounding procedure.

5.4   Problems with setup time

In this section we consider the multi-item, single machine problem with sequence independent setup costs, general production costs, and sequence independent setup times. Mathematically, this problem is formulated as:

$1/N/SI/G/SI$:

$$Z_{DLSP} = \min \sum_{i=1}^{N} \sum_{t=1}^{T} (S_i v_{i,t} + c_{i,t} y_{i,t}) - \sum_{i=1}^{N} \tilde{C}_i \qquad (5.8)$$

subject to

$$\sum_{\tau=1}^{t} y_{i,\tau} \geq D_{i,t} \qquad\qquad i = 1, .., N; \; t = 1, .., T-1 \quad (5.9a)$$

$$\sum_{\tau=1}^{T} y_{i,\tau} = D_{i,T} \qquad\qquad i = 1, .., N \qquad\qquad\qquad (5.9b)$$

$$\sum_{i=1}^{N} y_{i,t} + \sum_{i \in \mathcal{A}} v_{i,t} \leq 1 \qquad\qquad t = 1, .., T \qquad\qquad\qquad (5.10)$$

$$v_{i,t-a_i+\tau} \geq y_{i,t} - y_{i,t-1} \qquad\qquad i \in \mathcal{A}; \; t = a_i + 1, .., T; \qquad (5.11a)$$
$$\tau = 0, .., a_i - 1$$

$$v_{i,t} \geq y_{i,t} - y_{i,t-1} \qquad\qquad i \notin \mathcal{A}; \, t = 1, .., T \qquad (5.11b)$$

$$y_{i,t}, v_{i,t} \in \{0,1\} \qquad\qquad i = 1, .., N; \, t = 1, .., T \quad (5.12)$$

In the subsequent sections we describe two heuristics, based on column generation techniques, to solve this problem.

5.4.1 Column generation heuristics

As for the problem with zero setup times, the structure of DLSP with non zero setup times suggests a decomposition approach. The machine capacity constraints (5.10) complicate the solution by allowing at most one item to be setup or produced in any period. If we relax these constraints, using *non-positive* Lagrange multipliers $u = (u_1, \ldots, u_T)$, the Lagrangean problem LR(DLSP) can be stated as:

LR(DLSP)

$$Z_{LR(DLSP)}(u) \;\; = \;\; \min \sum_{i=1}^{N} \sum_{t=1}^{T} \left(S_i v_{i,t} + c_{i,t} y_{i,t} \right) +$$

$$+ \sum_{t=1}^{T} u_t \left(1 - \sum_{i=1}^{N} y_{i,t} - \sum_{i \in \mathcal{A}} v_{i,t} \right) \qquad (5.8')$$

subject to

(5.9), (5.11), (5.12)

Problem LR(DLSP) decomposes into N single item problems LR(DLSP)$_i$ $(i = 1, \ldots, N)$:

LR(DLSP)$_i$ $(i \in \mathcal{A})$

$$Z_{LR(DLSP)_i}(u) = \min \sum_{t=1}^{T} \left((S_i - u_t) \, v_{i,t} + (c_{i,t} - u_t) \, y_{i,t} \right) - \tilde{C}_i \quad (5.13)$$

subject to

$$D_{i,t} \leq \sum_{\tau=1}^{t} y_{i,\tau} \leq C'_{i,t} \qquad\qquad t = 1,..,T \qquad\qquad\qquad (5.14)$$

$$y_{i,t} + v_{i,t} \leq 1 \qquad\qquad t = 1,..,T \qquad\qquad\qquad (5.15)$$

$$v_{i,t-a_i+\tau} \geq y_{i,t} - y_{i,t-1} \qquad\qquad t = a_i+1,..,T; \tau = 0,..,a_i-1 \quad (5.16)$$

$$y_{i,t}, v_{i,t} \in \{0,1\} \qquad\qquad t = 1,..,T \qquad\qquad\qquad (5.17)$$

Finally, the constants $C'_{i,t}$ are upper bounds on the number of production periods for item i up to period t. These upper bounds account for the fact that capacity needs to be reserved for production and setup of other items. They are computed recursively as:

$$C'_{i,T} = D_{i,T}$$

and for $t = T - 1,..,1$

$$C'_{i,t} = \min(C'_{i,t+1}, \max(0, t - \sum_{j\neq i}(D_{j,t} + \delta(D_{j,t})a_j) - a_i))$$

where $\delta(x) = 1$ if $x > 0$ and $\delta(x) = 0$ otherwise.

For items $i \notin \mathcal{A}$ the term $(S_i - u_t)v_{i,t}$ in the objective function (5.13) is replaced by the term $S_i v_{i,t}$ while equations (5.15) are no longer valid and removed from the model formulation. Finally, equations (5.16) are replaced by $v_{i,t} \geq y_{i,t} - y_{i,t-1}$. Problems LR(DLSP)$_i$ are efficiently solved by Dynamic Programming, using an $\mathcal{O}(a_i D_{i,T} T)$ algorithm suggested in [95].

The questions that remain to be answered are:

- How to compute *strong* lower bounds, or equivalently, how to compute good values for the Lagrange multipliers u ? (Section 5.4.2)

- How to construct feasible solutions to DLSP ? (Section 5.4.3)

5.4.2 Lower bounding procedure

To compute values for the Lagrange multipliers u, we first discuss a column generation approach (see e.g. Lasdon [73]). The *master problem* is formulated as a Set Partitioning Problem (SPP):

SPP:

$$Z_{SPP} = \min \sum_{i=1}^{N} \left(\sum_{k=1}^{K_i} c_i^{(k)} x_i^{(k)} + M s_i \right) \tag{5.18}$$

subject to

$$\sum_{i=1}^{N} \sum_{k=1}^{K_i} a_{i,t}^{(k)} x_i^{(k)} \leq 1 \qquad\qquad t = 1,..,T \tag{5.19}$$

$$\sum_{k=1}^{K_i} x_i^{(k)} + s_i = 1 \qquad\qquad i = 1,..,N \tag{5.20}$$

$$x_i^{(k)}, s_i \in \{0,1\} \qquad\qquad i = 1,..,N; \ k = 1,..,K_i \tag{5.21}$$

In this model formulation superscripts k refer to the k-th production schedule added to SPP and K_i is the total number of production schedules added to SPP for item i. For the k-th production schedule, constants $c_i^{(k)}$ equal the cost of this schedule and constants $a_{i,t}^{(k)}$ are defined as:

$$a_{i,t}^{(k)} = \begin{cases} 1 & \text{if } y_{i,t} = 1 \text{ or } v_{i,t} = 1. \\ \\ 0 & \text{otherwise.} \end{cases}$$

Furthermore, decision variables $x_i^{(k)}$ are equal to one if for item i the k-th production schedule is implemented and zero otherwise. Slack variables s_i are introduced for item i to guarantee a feasible solution to the master problem. If $s_i = 1$, then Z_{SPP} is at least equal to some large penalty cost M and the solution to SPP does not contain a production schedule for item i. Consequently, the corresponding DLSP solution is infeasible. The objective (5.18) minimizes the sum of production cost and penalties. The set of constraints (5.19) state that in any period t at most one item is in production or in setup and equations (5.20) ensure that for each item either a production schedule is executed *or* a penalty M is added to the total cost. The binary character of the decision variables is represented by (5.21).

New columns (production schedules) for the master problem are generated by solving the Lagrangean subproblems LR(DLSP)$_i$ for each item $i = 1, \ldots, N$. It is a well-known result that when all feasible production schedules are generated, $Z_{SPP} = Z_{DLSP}$. However, the number of feasible production schedules may be prohibitively large and moreover, SPP is NP-Hard (see Garey and Johnson [44]). Therefore, we do not solve SPP but its Linear Programming relaxation LP(SPP). New production schedules are only added if they contribute to an improvement of the solution to LP(SPP), i.e. if they *price out*. To define this principle formally, let $w = (w_1, .., w_N)$ be the set of dual variables corresponding to equations (5.20) of LP(SPP). Then, a production schedule for item i prices out when $Z_{LR(DLSP)_i} < w_i$.

The procedure will be called Primal Column Generation Procedure (PCGP) because it solves the primal of LP(SPP). It can be summarized as follows:

Primal Column Generation Procedure (PCGP):

Step 1:   Generate for each item a number of feasible production schedules, using (randomization) heuristics.

Step 2:   Solve LP(SPP) and pass the dual variables u, corresponding to constraints (5.19), to the subproblems LR(DLSP)$_i$.

Step 3: Generate one new production schedule for each item i by solving LR(DLSP)$_i$ and add this production schedule to LP(SPP) if it prices out. If no production schedule prices out, then *STOP.* Otherwise, go to step 2.

For the relaxed problem LP(SPP) it is known that at the end of the column generation procedure $Z_{LP(SPP)} = \max_{u \leq 0} Z_{LR(DLSP)}(u)$ (see e.g. Fisher [39]). Although $Z_{LP(SPP)} \leq Z_{DLSP}$, it appears from computational results (see Section 5.5) that the LP-relaxation of SPP yields tight bounds quite often.

PCGP was first implemented in a straightforward way using the standard simplex method of LINDO (see Schrage [96]) to solve the master problem. However, since LP(SPP) is highly degenerate, CPU-times grow rapidly with problem size. In order to speed up this part of the algorithm, we suggest an alternative procedure to search for good values of the dual variables u. The procedure is based on solving the dual of problem LP(SPP), which is formulated as:

$LP(\widehat{SPP})$

$$Z_{LP(\widehat{SPP})} = \max \sum_{t=1}^{T} u_t + \sum_{i=1}^{N} w_i \qquad (5.22)$$

subject to

$$\sum_{t=1}^{T} a_{i,t}^{(k)} u_t + w_i \leq c_i^{(k)} \qquad\qquad i = 1, .., N; \; k = 1, .., K_i \quad (5.23)$$

$$u_t \leq 0 \qquad\qquad\qquad t = 1, .., T \qquad\qquad (5.24)$$

$$0 \leq w_i \leq M \qquad\qquad\qquad i = 1, .., N \qquad\qquad (5.25)$$

This problem is solved by a *dual ascent* heuristic. An extensive survey of dual ascent heuristics in combination with Lagrange relaxation

is given by Guignard and Rosenwein [53]. Our heuristic, which iteratively tries to increase several variables w while decreasing a single u
variable at a time, is described as follows:

Dual Ascent Procedure (Multiplier Adjustment Procedure):

Initialisation: Let dual variables u be predetermined and compute dual variables w as:

$$w_i = \begin{cases} 0 & \text{if } \delta_i < 0 \\ M & \text{if } \delta_i > M \\ \delta_i & \text{otherwise} \end{cases}$$

where

$\delta_i = \min_k \{ c_i^{(k)} - \sum_{t=1}^{T} a_{i,t}^{(k)} u_t \}$. Furthermore, let $\Delta_i^{(k)}$

be the slack variables corresponding to equations

(5.23), that is $\Delta_i^{(k)} = c_i^{(k)} - \sum_{t=1}^{T} a_{i,t}^{(k)} u_t - w_i$.

Step 1: Let $\mathcal{K}_{i,t}$ be the set of columns for which $a_{i,t}^{(k)} = 0$
and define $\mathcal{I}_t^{(1)} = \{i \mid K_{i,t} = \emptyset\}$.

Compute $\alpha_{i,t} = \min_{\mathcal{K}_{i,t}} \Delta_i^{(k)}$ and let $\mathcal{I}_t^{(2)}$ be the set of
items for which $\alpha_{i,t} > 0$.

Set $\beta_t = \min[\min_{i \in \mathcal{I}_t^{(1)}} \{M - w_i\}, \min_{i \in \mathcal{I}_t^{(2)}} \{\alpha_{i,t}, M - w_i\}]$.

Let $\mathcal{I}_t = \mathcal{I}_t^{(1)} \cup \mathcal{I}_t^{(2)}$ and determine
$t^* = \arg\max_t \beta_t(|\mathcal{I}_t| - 1)$

Step 2: Update $u_{t^*} := u_{t^*} - \beta_{t^*}$ and $w_i := w_i + \beta_{t^*}$ for all
$i \in \mathcal{I}_{t^*}$. Moreover, update slack variables $\Delta_i^{(k)} :=$
$\Delta_i^{(k)} - \beta_{t^*}$ for all $i \in \mathcal{I}_{t^*}$ and $k \in \mathcal{K}_{i,t^*}$. If $\beta_{t^*} > 0$
go to Step 1, otherwise STOP.

Since the dual ascent procedure does not usually reach the LP-optimum, we attempt to improve the lower bound by applying *subgradient optimization*. The dual variables u are updated during a fixed number of iterations according to the following formula:

$$u_t := \min(0, u_t + \lambda(1 - \sum_{i=1}^{N} \sum_{k=1}^{K_i} a_{i,t}^{(k)} x_i^{(k)})) \quad \text{for } t = 1, .., T$$

where λ is a positive scalar step size, determined as:

$$\lambda = \frac{\omega(UB - LB)}{\sum_{t=1}^{T} \left(1 - \sum_{i=1}^{N} \sum_{k=1}^{K_i} a_{i,t}^{(k)} x_i^{(k)}\right)^2}$$

The scalar ω is initialized at 1.5 and halved whenever the lower bound has failed to increase for some fixed number of iterations. The initial lower bound (LB) is given by the (heuristic) solution to $LP(\widehat{SPP})$, while the upper bound (UB) is given by the best known solution to DLSP so far (UB is initialized at an appropriate large number). During the subgradient optimization procedure, new solutions (and lower bounds) to SPP are obtained by solving the Lagrange Relaxation of SPP (LR(SPP)), which is formulated as:

LR(SPP)

$$Z_{LR(SPP)}(u) = \min \sum_{i=1}^{N} (\sum_{k=1}^{K_i} (c_i^{(k)} - \sum_{t=1}^{T} a_{i,t}^{(k)} u_t) x_i^{(k)} + M s_i) + \sum_{t=1}^{T} u_t \quad (5.24)$$

subject to

(5.20), (5.21)

Note that LR(SPP) is solved by simple inspection using the rule:

$$x_i^{(k)} = \begin{cases} 1 & \text{if } \min_\ell \{c_i^{(\ell)} - \sum_{t=1}^{T} a_{i,t}^{(\ell)} u_t\} < M \text{ and} \\ & \text{this minimum is obtained for } \ell = k. \\ \\ 0 & \text{otherwise.} \end{cases}$$

and $s_i = 1$ if $x_i^{(k)} = 0$ for all $k = 1, .., K_i$ and $s_i = 0$ otherwise.

The Dual Column Generation Procedure (DCGP) can be summarized as follows:

Dual Column Generation Procedure (DCGP):

Step 1: Generate for each item a number of feasible production schedules, using (randomization) heuristics. Set $u_t = 0$ for $t = 1, .., T$.

Step 2: Solve $LP(\widehat{SPP})$ by dual ascent, starting with dual variables u obtained in the preceding iteration. Then apply I^{max} iterations of the subgradient optimization. Pass on the (approximately optimal) dual variables u to the subproblems LR(DLSP)$_i$.

Step 3: Generate one new production schedule for each item i by solving $LR(DLSP)_i$ and add this production schedule to $LP(\widehat{SPP})$ if it prices out. If no production schedule prices out, then *STOP*. Otherwise go to step 2.

5.4.3 Upper bounding procedure

The question that remains to be answered is how to find *feasible* solutions to DLSP, or equivalently, how to generate strong upper bounds (UB). If we use PCGP, every integer solution to LP(SPP) is clearly an upper bound. However, although the columns obtained by PCGP may contain an integer solution, it is not necessarily found by the simplex algorithm. To overcome this difficulty, the integer program SPP is solved after termination of the column generation procedure, using the branch and bound procedure of LINDO. Note that this procedure does not guarantee an integer feasible solution, since the IP only contains the columns generated by PCGP (i.e. a subset of all possible columns). Therefore, although the DLSP at hand may be feasible, the SPP defined on the columns generated by PCGP may very well contain no integer feasible solution.

Finding feasible solutions to DLSP using DCGP is done in two different ways. First, in step 2 an integer solution to LR(SPP) may be found in which $s_i = 0$ for $i = 1, .., N$ and the slacks corresponding to (5.19) are all non-negative. Clearly, this solution is also feasible to DLSP. Second, we try to find feasible solutions among the columns generated so far, by solving SPP using the enumeration algorithm of Garfinkel and Nemhauser [45]. This algorithm is executed every ten iterations *after step 3* of DCGP.

In case of *zero setup times*, we have extended PCGP and DCGP with an effective upper bounding procedure developed by Fleischmann [40] as described in Section 5.3, which guarantees a feasible starting solution.

Remark: When setup times are nonzero, the existence of a simple feasibility rule is unlikely (remember that generating feasible schedules in presence of nonzero setup times is NP-Complete) and Fleischmann's procedure cannot be used anymore. Therefore we were forced to test other procedures. We have chosen for the column generation approach, since this technique has the appealing property that the probability of generating a feasible solution is rather high (see Ryan and Falkner [93]).

5.5   Computational results

The heuristics PCGP and DCGP were programmed in FORTRAN and implemented on an IBM-PS 2 Model 80 with mathematical co-processor 80386. Test problems were generated using a problem generator which is available upon request. Variations in the following problem parameters were considered:

- The problem dimensions, as represented by the number of items N and the number of periods T.

- The setup times, which are either constant or generated at random from a discrete uniform (DU) distribution.

- The (approximate) EOQ-based time between ordering for item i, (TBO_i), which is randomly generated from a discrete uniform distribution.

- The (approximate) capacity utilization ρ and demand $d_{i,t}$, so that:

$$Prob\ \{\ d_{i,t} = 1\ \} = \frac{\rho}{N}\ \left(1 - \frac{a_i}{TBO_i}\right)$$

Demand for item i in period t is set equal to one whenever $U \leq Prob\{\ d_{i,t} = 1\ \}$ and set equal to zero otherwise. (Here, U is generated randomly from a uniform $U(0,1)$ distribution.) During the generation of demand for period t it is checked whether $D_{i,t} \leq C'_{i,t}$ holds for $i = 1,..,N$. If this *rough cut capacity check* is violated for some item i, demand for period t is regenerated for all items.

Two sets of test problems were generated. The first set consists of 45 $1/N/SI/G/A$ problems (*zero* setup times) while the second set contains 420 $1/N/SI/G/SI$ problems (*nonzero* setup times). For both sets of test problems, the following parameters have been fixed: the machine speed $r_i = 1$, the holding cost $h_i = 1$, the production cost $p_{i,t} = 0$ ($t = 1,..,T$) and the setup cost $S_i = D_{i,T} \times TBO_i^2/2T$ for $i = 1,..,N$. Furthermore, after some preliminary experiments with DCGP, the maximum number of subgradient iterations (I^{max}) has been fixed at 100 for all test problems.

1/N/SI/G/A problems.

This set of test problems consists of 60 period problems with $N = 2$, $N = 4$, and $N = 6$ items respectively. For each item-period combination we consider low (L) capacitated problems ($\rho \leq 0.55$), medium (M) capacitated problems ($0.55 < \rho \leq 0.75$) and high (H) capacitated problems ($\rho > 0.75$) with $TBO_i \sim DU(12,20)$ for $i = 1,..,N$. Per (N,ρ)

combination five problems were generated, resulting in $(3 \times 3) \times 5 = 45$ problems. All problems in this set were solved using three solution procedures: Fleischmann's heuristic (*before* entering the branch and bound phase), PCGP and DCGP.

Table 5.1 shows the results for the first set of test problems. Here, the quality of the solutions is represented by *the gap* $\overline{\Delta Z}$, which is the average relative deviation (in percent) between upper bound (UB) and lower bound (LB), computed as: $\overline{\Delta Z} = 100\% \times (UB - LB)/LB$ over all solutions within each (N, ρ) combination. Furthermore, for each combination the total number of problems solved to *optimality* $(\overline{\Delta Z} = 0)$ is denoted by O and the number of problems with a *positive gap* $(\overline{\Delta Z} > 0)$ is denoted by G. The average CPU time (in seconds) is denoted by $\overline{CPU}$.

Table 5.1. Computational results for 1/N/SI/G/A problems.

		Fleischmann				PCGP				DCGP			
N	ρ	$\overline{\Delta Z}$	O	G	$\overline{CPU}$	$\overline{\Delta Z}$	O	G	$\overline{CPU}$	$\overline{\Delta Z}$	O	G	$\overline{CPU}$
	L	0.13	4	1	< 1.0	0.00	5	0	26.2	0.40	4	1	7.0
2	M	0.11	4	1	2.6	0.00	5	0	1784.9	0.00	5	0	20.2
	H	0.33	3	2	< 1.0			(^{1}		0.04	4	1	17.0
	L	0.40	3	2	1.6	0.00	5	0	14.6	0.00	5	0	21.6
4	M	0.42	3	2	3.4	0.07	3	2	206.6	0.07	3	2	39.6
	H	0.24	3	2	5.6			(^{1}		0.10	4	1	106.0
	L	0.50	3	2	2.0	0.00	5	0	27.2	0.00	5	0	38.2
6	M	0.58	0	5	7.8	0.74	2	3	658.2	0.14	4	1	77.0
	H	0.62	1	4	5.8			(^{1}		0.00	5	0	92.6

(^{1}: LINDO was not able to solve problems in this problem class.

Evaluating the results, it can be seen that Fleischmann's heuristic finds an optimal solution for 24 out of 45 problems (53 %), while this percentage is 83 % (out of 30 problems) and 86 % for PCGP and DCGP respectively. The average gap $(\overline{\Delta Z})$ for the solutions found by Fleischmann's heuristic amounts to 0.37 %, while for PCGP and DCGP the gap is 0.14 % (30 problems) and 0.08 % respectively. Computation times for Fleischmann and for DCGP increase in most (but not all) cases when capacity utilization increases and when the number of items grows larger. The CPU-time required to solve problems using PCGP grows rapidly when capacity utilization increases. In fact, highly capacitated problems (H) could not be solved because degeneracy made the number of columns generated too large to be handled by LINDO.

Computation times for the column generation based heuristics PCGP and DCGP turn out to be rather large compared to Fleischmann's heuristic. This is caused by the fact that PCGP and DCGP were developed for problems with *nonzero* setup times, and therefore consist of effective, but time and memory consuming procedures for finding feasible production schedules. These procedures obviously do not fully exploit the structure of problems with zero setup times as Fleischmann's procedure does.

Problems with setup times.

The second set of test problems consists of the following item-period combinations: $\{(N,T) \mid (2,20),\ (2,40),\ (2,60),\ (4,40),\ (4,60),\ (6,60)\}$. Setup time for item i is generated as $a_i \sim DU(0,2)$ and time between ordering is either low (L) ($TBO_i \sim DU(8,16)$), medium (M) ($TBO_i \sim DU(12,20)$) or high (H) ($TBO_i \sim DU(20,30)$). For 20-period problems only low TBO's are considered and for 40-period problems high TBO's are left out. For each item-period combination we have again generated low (L), medium (M) and high (H) capacitated problems.
In total we consider 42 different (N,T,TBO,ρ) combinations. For each of these combinations 10 different data sets were generated, yielding a total of 420 problems. Since the first set of test problems shows that DCGP largely outperforms PCGP with respect to computation times, results for the second set of test problems relate to DCGP only, unless stated otherwise. Furthermore, because computational results for different TBO classes differ only slightly, we aggregate results over all TBO's. (The latter causes an unequal number of problems within each (N,T,ρ) class.)

Computational results are given in Tables 5.2 and 5.3.

The notation in Table 5.2 is analogous to the one used in Table 5.1, except that gap $(\overline{\Delta Z})$ is computed over all *feasible* solutions within each (N,T,ρ) combination. In addition, the number of problems for which no feasible integer solution was found by DCGP are denoted by I. If no feasible integer solution for a particular problem instance is found by DCGP, an attempt is made to solve the problem by PCGP. If a feasible integer solution is found by PCGP, this is denoted by ([1]. Problems for which the LP-relaxation of SPP (LP(SPP)) is feasible, but for which no feasible integer solution is found are denoted by ([2]. All other problem instances in the category I turn out to be infeasible with respect to LP(SPP).

Table 5.2. Computational results for 1/N/SI/G/SI problems solved by DCGP.

N	ρ	$\overline{\Delta Z}$	O	G	I	$\overline{\Delta Z}$	O	G	I	$\overline{\Delta Z}$	O	G	I
		\multicolumn{4}{T=20}				$T=40$				$T=60$		
	L	0.00	10	0	0	0.09	19	1	0	0.17	25	3	2
2	M	0.29	7	1	2	0.06	15	1	4	0.20	21	2	7
	H	0.86	5	1	4	0.01	13	1	6	1.22	10	10	10
	L					0.00	19	0	1	0.15	23	4	3
4	M					0.15	12	3	([1] 5	0.47	19	5	6
	H					0.96	7	4	9	1.43	14	5	([2] 11
	L									0.13	26	3	1
6	M									0.70	13	7	([1] 10
	H									0.99	11	9	10

([1]: Feasible integer solution found by PCGP for one problem instance.
([2]: LP-relaxation is feasible but no integer solution found by PCGP for one problem instance.

Examination of the computational results shows that $\overline{\Delta Z}$ tends to increase when capacity utilization increases and when the number of periods increases. For low capacitated problems $\overline{\Delta Z}$ ranges from 0% to 0.17% while for high capacitated problems the gap turns out to be lower than 1.43%. This demonstrates that lower bounds obtained by fast heuristic methods like dual ascent and subgradient optimization are rather tight for DLSP. Considering the low capacitated problems it can be seen that only 11 out of 133 feasible problems have a gap, while for the medium and high capacitated problems these numbers are 19 out of 106 and 30 out of 90 respectively. It is remarkable that only for 3 out of 329 feasible problem instances no integer solution was found by DCGP, while it did find an optimal solution to 269 problems. This demonstrates that the upper bounding procedures are quite effective, especially for the relatively easy low capacitated problems.

Table 5.3. Computational results for 1/N/SI/G/SI problems solved by DCGP.

		$T = 20$			$T = 40$			$T = 60$		
N	ρ	F	B	C	F	B	C	F	B	C
	L	0.3	0.9	1.9	1.1	4.7	8.6	4.1	12.8	25.8
2	M	0.3	1.8	2.4	6.8	14.7	20.4	13.9	36.2	76.3
	H	0.8	5.1	8.8	22.7	65.6	93.6	69.5	188.6	274.9
	L				2.8	9.7	15.9	9.1	30.6	38.9
4	M				8.9	25.7	37.8	68.4	107.1	120.8
	H				48.7	61.8	79.5	178.4	231.8	268.7
	L							17.6	38.8	56.2
6	M							95.7	144.9	264.9
	H							142.7	209.5	274.1

Table 5.3 shows CPU-times (in seconds) for each (N,T,ρ) combination. Here, F is the average time (over all LP-feasible problems) required to find the *first* integer solution, B is the average time (again, over all LP-feasible problems) after which the *best* integer solution is found and C is the average time (over *all* problems) required for DCGP.

As can be seen from the results in Table 5.3, computation times grow with problem size, which can be explained by the fact that solving N single item subproblems takes $\mathcal{O}(\sum_{i=1}^{N} a_i D_{i,T} T)$ per iteration. Furthermore, computation times increase when capacity utilization increases. The reason for this is that for high capacitated problems more columns have to be generated on average in order to obtain a feasible solution. Consequently, solving SPP by the enumeration algorithm of Garfinkel and Nemhauser takes longer. Nevertheless, considering the complexity of problems with nonzero setup times, computation times are fairly modest. Small problems (2 items and 20 periods) are solved in a few seconds, while medium sized problems (6 items and 60 periods) are solved within five minutes (on average).

5.6 Summary and discussion

In this chapter a number of algorithms for solving multi-item DLSP problems were discussed. Exact solution procedures based on dynamic programming as presented in Section 5.2 appeared to be too time and memory consuming to be effective for solving other than toy sized problems. As an alternative to these exact procedures, the heuristic proposed by Fleischmann for problem $1/N/SI/G/A$ (Section 5.3.1) seemed to be very effective, even for larger problems. An extension of this algorithm to problem $1/N/SD/G/A$ as proposed by Fleischmann and Popp [41] does not perform very well, due to the poor quality of the lower bounds, which may be caused by the transformation of setup costs. In Section 5.4 a primal (PCGP) and a dual (DCGP) column generation heuristic were presented for problem $1/N/SI/G/SI$. These heuristics represent one of the very few efforts at solving lot sizing problems with setup times. Computational results on a set of 420 problems show that for some 82% of these problems an optimal solution is found, while in most other cases feasible solutions are found whose deviation from optimality is no more than 1.5% (on average). For medium sized problems (6 items and 60 periods) solutions are obtained on a personal computer within 5 minutes of CPU-time.

From a computational comparison between Fleischmann's heuristic, PCGP and DCGP on a set of 45 $1/N/SI/G/A$ problems it appears that Fleischmann's heuristic largely outperforms the column generation heuristics in computational speed, but that solutions obtained by the column generation heuristics are slightly better in quality.
Note that Fleischmann's special purpose algorithm takes advantage of the structure of the problem without setup times, while ours does not.

This explains the differences in computational requirements.

The results for DCGP are encouraging when compared to computational results obtained for other capacitated lotsizing models *with* setup times (like The Capacitated Lotsizing Problem, considered by Trigeiro et al. [101]). The reasons for this are twofold: First, DLSP is one of the few multi-item capacitated lotsizing problem formulations for which the capacitated single item subproblems resulting from relaxation of the multi-item capacity constraints are polynomially solvable and second, the (Lagrangean) lower bounds obtained in this way turn out to be rather tight for most problem instances. For generating upper bounds, application of a column generation heuristic in combination with the fast enumeration algorithm of Garfinkel and Nemhauser performs quite satisfactorily, since the probability of finding feasible (integer) solutions to DLSP turns out to be rather high.

Chapter 6

The Uncapacitated Problem

6.1 Introduction

In this chapter we consider the uncapacitated version of the Multilevel Lotsizing Problem (MLLP). The MLLP is the problem of determining a time-phased production schedule for a production process characterized by multilevel product structures, such that total relevant costs are minimized and demand is fulfilled without backlogging.

Typically, in a multilevel product structure two types of demand occur: *independent* demand, which is the demand from outside the firm (e.g. customer demand), and *dependent* demand, which is the demand for components, triggered by the production required to fulfil the independent demand. Independent demand is assumed to be known in consecutive time periods up to some fixed planning horizon.

The relevant costs considered in MLLP consist of machine setup costs, inventory holding costs and production costs. Machine setup costs are incurred whenever production takes place in a planning period, independent of the occurrence of a setup in a preceding planning period (this contrasts to the Discrete Lotsizing and Scheduling Problem, discussed in Chapters 3,4, and 5). Inventory holding costs are proportional to the inventory positions at the end of planning periods. Production costs considered in MLLP may be time-dependent and are proportional to the amount produced per period.

Finally, like in most MRP systems (see Chapter 1), it is assumed that production capacity is *infinitely* available in each planning period.

The difficulties in MLLP are caused by the complex interdependencies which (may) exist between planning decisions for different items. These interdependencies in the product structure will be described by (integer) numbers $g_{i,j}$, where i and j range over all item numbers. The meaning of the *gozinto factors* $g_{i,j}$ is that the production of one unit of j requires input of $g_{i,j}$ units of item i.

One can associate with a product structure an acyclic graph where each item i defines a vertex i in the graph and an arc starting in i and ending in j is present whenever $g_{i,j} > 0$. We assume that all items are numbered such that $g_{i,j} = 0$ when $j \geq i$. Figure 6.1 shows an example of a product structure depicted as an acyclic graph.

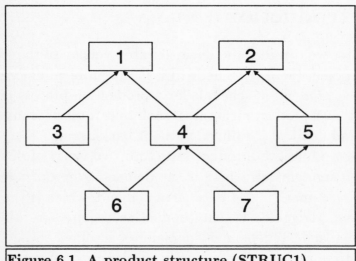

Figure 6.1. A product structure (STRUC1).

When considering two items i and j with $g_{i,j} > 0$, then item i is termed a *predecessor* of item j and item j is called a *successor* of item i. From now on we will denote the set of all predecessors of item i by $\mathcal{P}_i$ and the set of all successors of item i by $\mathcal{S}_i$. In general we distinguish between four type of product structures:

- A *serial* product structure, in which each item has at most one predecessor and one successor

- An *assembly* product structure, where each item has at most one successor.

- An *arborescent* product structure, where each item has at most one predecessor.

- Finally, a product structure is named *general* if it cannot be classified into one of the other categories (i.e. when items exist for which the number of predecessors and successors is greater than one).

The *level* number of an item is a (nonnegative) integer and can be defined recursively as follows: An item is defined to have level number ℓ if the item is direct input for an item with level number $\ell - 1$. End items, by convention, are assigned a level number of 0. The *depth* of a product structure is the maximum level number which occurs. In the example of Figure 6.1 the depth is 2 (although the *number* of levels equals three).

Mathematically, MLLP can be defined as the following mixed-integer linear program:

MLLP:

$$Z_{MLLP} = \min \sum_{i=1}^{N} \sum_{t=1}^{T} \left(S_i y_{i,t} + h_i I_{i,t} + p_{i,t} x_{i,t} \right) \tag{6.1}$$

subject to

$$I_{i,t-1} + x_{i,t-L_i} - \sum_{j \in S_i} g_{i,j} x_{j,t} - d_{i,t} = I_{i,t} \quad i = 1, .., N;\, t = 1, .., T \tag{6.2}$$

$$x_{i,t} \leq M y_{i,t} \qquad\qquad\qquad i = 1, .., N;\, t = 1, .., T \tag{6.3}$$

$$x_{i,t} \geq 0 \qquad\qquad\qquad i = 1, .., N;\, t = 1, .., T \tag{6.4}$$

$$I_{i,t} \geq 0 \qquad\qquad\qquad i = 1, .., N;\, t = 1, .., T \tag{6.5}$$

$$y_{i,t} \in \{0, 1\} \qquad\qquad\qquad i = 1, .., N;\, t = 1, .., T \tag{6.6}$$

Parameters in the model are:

T =   the number of planning periods (planning horizon).

N =   the total number of items in the production process.

$d_{i,t}$ =   (independent) demand in period t for item i.

$g_{i,j}$ =   the number of units required as input from item i to make one unit of item j (gozinto factors).

$\mathcal{P}_i$ =   the set of all predecessor items of item i.

$\mathcal{S}_i$ =   the set of all successor items of item i.

S_i =   the setup cost for production of item i.

h_i =   the holding cost per period and per unit of inventory for item i.

$p_{i,t}$ =   the production cost for item i in period t.

L_i =   (integer) production lead time of item i.

M =   some large number.

Decision variables in the model are:

$x_{i,t}$ =   production quantity for item i in period t.

$y_{i,t}$ =   binary variable which takes the value 1 if a setup is made for item i in period t and zero otherwise.

$I_{i,t}$ =   inventory position for item i at the end of period t.

The objective function (6.1) states that setup, production, and inventory variables have to be determined such that the sum of setup costs, inventory holding costs and production costs is minimized. The minimal total cost of a production schedule is given by Z_{MLLP}. Constraints (6.2) to (6.6) express the restrictions imposed on the solutions of the model. The constraint set (6.2) states the balance between production, independent demand, dependent demand, and end-of-period inventory for each item-period combination. In the sequel we assume (without loss of generality) production lead time $L_i = 0$ for all items i. Coupling between production and setup variables is forced by constraints (6.3).

For an appropriate choice of the constant M, these constraints precisely implement the logical restriction that production for item i in period t (i.e. $x_{i,t} > 0$) can only take place when a set-up is scheduled, i.e., when $y_{i,t} = 1$. Constraint (6.4) states the obvious condition that production quantities are non-negative, while the non-negativity of end-of-period inventory expressed in the constraint set (6.5) implies that no backlogging is allowed in satisfying demand. Finally, the constraint set (6.6) expresses the binary character of setup decisions.

Research on MLLP was initiated by Zangwill [112] (1966), Veinott [104] (1969), and Love [76] (1972). These authors stress the point that MLLP is not only a "hard" problem from a theoretical point of view (for general product structures the problem has been proved to be NP-Hard (see Arkin et al. [6]), but that it is also difficult to handle from a computational point of view. Besides the already indicated difficulties due to complex interdependencies in the product structure, additional difficulties are caused by the poor quality of lower bounds obtained by straightforward relaxation of the integrality constraints (6.6) on set-up variables. This makes it impossible to solve MLLP using general purpose branch-and-bound routines as provided by e.g. LINDO, even for smaller sized problem instances (upto 6 items and 12 planning periods). Therefore, we are committed to specialized algorithms which exploit the structure of the constraint matrix of MLLP more explicitly. Most progress in solving MLLP has been achieved for special cases, in particular serial and assembly systems. Among the first to research serial and assembly systems were Crowston and Wagner [26]. Inspired by the so-called *"nesting"* property discovered by Love [76] (see also Section 6.2), they proposed the use of a dynamic programming approach. However, the computational effort increases exponentially with the number of planning periods, thereby rendering the method inefficient for larger problems. A recent method (1984) for solving assembly problems was suggested by Afentakis, Gavish and Karmarkar [3]. Their main contribution was the transformation of the constraint matrix of MLLP into an equivalent matrix with a block diagonal structure linked by a set of coupling constraints. After relaxation of the coupling constraints, the dependent demand for each item becomes independent of the production for items situated at lower levels (i.e. higher numbered levels) in the product structure. The natural decomposition of the problem then leads to a set of single-item production planning problems linked by a set of Lagrange multipliers. The single item production planning problems can be solved efficiently using a shortest path algorithm. The lower bounds obtained in this way have been incorporated into a specialized branch-and-bound algorithm. Upper bounds are computed using a number of simple heuristics. The algorithm assumes however that independent demand exists for *end-items* (level 0) *only* and that production costs are *constant* over time. In addition, *zero starting inventories* are assumed for all items. Computational experiments have shown that the method is capable of solving assembly MLLP's consisting of 40 items and 12 periods in roughly 20 seconds (CPU time) on an IBM 3032 computer.

An alternative algorithm for solving assembly problems was developed by Rosling [92] in 1985. This algorithm is based on a reformulation of the original assembly MLLP into a facility location related problem. An appropriate relaxation of this reformulation yields single-item facility location problems, which are solved effectively using a dual algorithm. Computational experiments have shown that this relaxation, in combination with a cross decomposition technique, leads to sharp bounds for MLLP.

In a subsequent paper (1986), Afentakis and Gavish [2] extend their method presented in [3] to general product structures. This method is based on a transformation of the general product structure into an equivalent and larger assembly structure. Lagrangean relaxation of coupling constraints yields easily solved shortest path problems. Upper bounds are obtained by using partial enumeration heuristics. Nevertheless, the suggested method is still not able to deal with independent demand for other than end-items, time dependent production costs or nonzero starting inventories. Furthermore, a computational study on a set of test problems shows that computational requirements grow rapidly with the number of items and with the number of levels in the product structure.

For MLLP with general product structures several heuristics have been proposed. Often, these heuristics are based on a decomposition of MLLP into single-level subproblems, in combination with cost adaptation procedures, which account for interactions between adjacent levels

(like e.g. the heuristics developed by Blackburn and Millen [18]).
Kuik and Salomon [69] suggest a different approach, based on a statistical search technique, called *simulated annealing*. Although the method proposed in [69] is applicable to more general problems than the method suggested in [2] (in that it allows for independent demand for components and time-dependent production costs), a disadvantage is that computational requirements grow rapidly when the problem size increases. We will refrain from a further discussion of statistical search techniques here, since they are considered in more detail in Section 7.2.

In this chapter we present a new heuristic for solving general MLLP's. The heuristic is based on a Lagrangean decomposition of MLLP, which yields lower bounds. To obtain upper bounds, a cost adaptation heuristic is used. A comprehensive explanation of this procedure is found in Section 6.2. Computational results on a set of randomly generated test problems are reported in Section 6.3. Finally, a summary and some conclusions are given in Section 6.4.

6.2 A simple decomposition heuristic

The heuristic presented in this section is based on a decomposition approach which consists of the following steps:

- Elimination of inventory variables from MLLP, by substitution of the balance equations (6.2) in the objective function (6.1).

- Lagrangean relaxation of the non-negativity conditions imposed on inventory variables, as stated by condition (6.5).

Upon execution of these steps, the remaining "Lagrangean" problem LR(MLLP) decomposes into N single-item lotsizing problems, which can be formulated for each item i as:

$LR(MLLP)_i$

$$Z_{LR(MLLP)_i}(u) = \min \sum_{t=1}^{T} \left(S_i y_{i,t} + c_{i,t} x_{i,t} \right) \tag{6.7}$$

subject to

(6.3), (6.4), (6.6)

where $u = \{u_{i,t}\}_{i,t}$ is a set of non-positive Lagrange multipliers, and constants $c_{i,t}$ are given by:

$$c_{i,t} = \left(h_i - \sum_{j \in \mathcal{P}_i} g_{j,i} h_j \right) (T - t + 1) + \sum_{\tau=t}^{T} \left(u_{i,\tau} - \sum_{j \in \mathcal{P}_i} g_{j,i} u_{j,\tau} \right) + p_{i,t}$$

Computation of lower bounds.

Lower bounds are now obtained by adding additional constraints to LR(MLLP)$_i$. These constraints are based on a natural *explosion* of dependent demand. The so-called "exploded demand" $\tilde{d}_{i,t}$ is computed for each item $i = 1, .., N$, using the following recursion:

$$\tilde{d}_{i,t} = d_{i,t} + \sum_{j \in \mathcal{S}_i} g_{i,j} \tilde{d}_{j,t}$$

The constraints added to LR(MLLP)$_i$ are simple one-item balance equations of the form:

$$\sum_{\tau=1}^{t} x_{i,\tau} \geq \sum_{\tau=1}^{t} \tilde{d}_{i,\tau} \qquad \qquad \text{for } i = 1, .., N; \; t = 1, .., T \quad (6.8)$$

Note that the total cost of subproblems, consisting of the objective function (6.7) and constraints (6.3), (6.4), (6.6) and (6.8) yield a lower bound. The subproblems are solved efficiently in $\mathcal{O}(T^2)$ by the well-known Wagner-Whitin algorithm [107] or in $\mathcal{O}(T \log T)$, applying the recently developed algorithm by Wagelmans et al. [106]. Under certain assumptions with respect to the input parameters, lower bounds can even be tightened using the so-called *nesting* property, which is stated in the following lemma.

Lemma 6.1 (Nesting Property) *If independent demand occurs for end-items only, and if production costs are constant over time, then there exists an optimal solution to MLLP for which $y_{i,t} = 0$ whenever $\sum_{j \in \mathcal{S}_i} y_{j,t} = 0$.*

Proof: See Afentakis and Gavish [2]. □

As a result of this lemma, the constraint set $y_{i,t} \leq \sum_{j \in \mathcal{S}_i} y_{j,t}$ can be added to LR(DLSP)$_i$. However, by doing so, we would disturb the (single-item) structure of the sub-problems. Therefore, we add these restrictions in a "Lagrangean" way to the objective function (6.7), which results in the following objective:

$$Z_{LR(MLLP)_i}(u, v) = \min \sum_{t=1}^{T} \left(S_i' y_{i,t} + c_{i,t} x_{i,t} \right) \tag{6.7'}$$

where S_i' is given by:

$$S_i' = \begin{cases} S_i + \sum_{j \in \mathcal{P}_i} v_{j,t} & \text{if } |\mathcal{S}_i| = 0 \\[2mm] S_i - v_{i,t} + \sum_{j \in \mathcal{P}_i} v_{j,t} & \text{otherwise} \end{cases}$$

and $v = \{v_{i,t}\}_{i,t}$ is a set of non-positive Lagrange multipliers.

Computation of upper bounds.

Upper bounds are computed analogously to lower bounds, that is, by sequentially solving single-item problems, except that balance equations (6.8) are replaced by equations (6.8'):

$$\sum_{\tau=1}^{t} x_{i,\tau} \geq \sum_{\tau=1}^{t} \tilde{x}_{i,\tau} \qquad \text{for } i = 1, .., N; \; t = 1, .., T \tag{6.8'}$$

where $\tilde{x}_{i,t}$ is the *exploded production*, computed recursively as $\tilde{x}_{i,t} = d_{i,t} + \sum_{j \in \mathcal{S}_i} g_{i,j} \tilde{x}_{j,t}$. Note that, by solving problems consisting of the objective (6.7) and constraints (6.3), (6.4), (6.6) and (6.8'), we will ultimately end-up with a feasible solution with respect to equations

(6.2) to (6.6). Such a solution is clearly an upper bound to MLLP. If the nesting property holds, an attempt can be made to improve upper bounds by adding restrictions of the form $x_{i,t} \leq M \sum_{j \in S_i} \tilde{x}_{j,t}$ to LR(DLSP)$_i$. These restrictions are easily incorporated into the dynamic program for solving the single-item subproblems, and do not alter computational complexity.

Our MLLP heuristic (MLLPH) can be summarized as follows:

MLLPH:

Initialization: Compute exploded demand $\tilde{d}_{i,t}$ and put $u_{i,t} = 0$ for all items i and periods t.

Step 1: Compute lower bounds (using one's own favourite single-item algorithm) by solving for each item sub-problems consisting of (6.7), (6.3), (6.4), (6.6) and (6.8).

Step 2: Sequentially compute for each item exploded production $\tilde{x}_{i,t}$ and solve the problem consisting of (6.7), (6.3), (6.4) (6.6) and (6.8') (again, using one's own favourite single-item algorithm). Substitution of setup variables $y_{i,t}$, and production variables $x_{i,t}$ in (6.1), yields new upper bounds.

Step 3: If the maximum number of iterations (I^{max}) is reached, or the gap between lower bound and upper bound is smaller than a prespecified constant ϵ, then STOP. Otherwise, update Lagrange multipliers $u_{i,t}$, using *subgradient optimization* (see Section 5.4) and go to step 1.

For problem instances for which the nesting property holds (Lemma 6.1), the objective function $(6.7')$ is used instead of (6.7) in steps 1 and 2. In this case, dual variables $v_{i,t}$ are initialized and updated analogously to dual variables $u_{i,t}$. Furthermore, restrictions of the form $x_{i,t} \leq M \sum_{j \in S_i} \tilde{x}_{j,t}$ are added to the single-item subproblems when determining upper bounds in step 2. In what follows, we denote $MLLPH$, adapted in the above mentioned way, as $\overline{MLLPH}$.

6.3 Computational Results

The heuristic MLLPH was programmed in TURBO-Pascal (Version 5.0) and implemented on an Olivetti M380/XP3 with mathematical co-processor 30387. Test problems are generated for four product structures, with a different number of items, dependencies and levels. These product structures are subsequently denoted by STRUC1, STRUC2, STRUC3 and STRUC4. All nonzero gozinto factors $(g_{i,j})$ are assumed to be equal to one. Product structure STRUC1 is shown in Figure 6.1, while the other product structures are depicted in Figure 6.2.

We consider for each product structure two different sets of test problems. The *first set* of test problems, denoted by Set I, consists of instances with independent demand for end-items *only*, while the *second set* of test problems, denoted by Set II, consists of instances with independent demand for *all* items. For all test problems the number of planning periods equals twelve $(T = 12)$ and in each period the independent demand for *end-items* is generated randomly from a normal distribution with an average of 20 and a standard deviation of 5. For instances from Set II, independent demand $d_{i,t}$ for *component i* in period t is taken to be equal to zero with probability p, and with probability $1-p$ generated randomly from a normal distribution with an average of 20 and a standard deviation of 5. In our experiments we have set p equal to 0.75. The holding costs for item i are obtained from the so-called *echelon holding costs* $(\tilde{h}_i)$, which are defined as $\tilde{h}_i = h_i - \sum_{j \in \mathcal{P}_i} g_{j,i} h_j$. Echelon holding costs are generated randomly from a uniform distribution with minimum 0.3 and maximum 0.5. Setup costs are computed using the following relation:

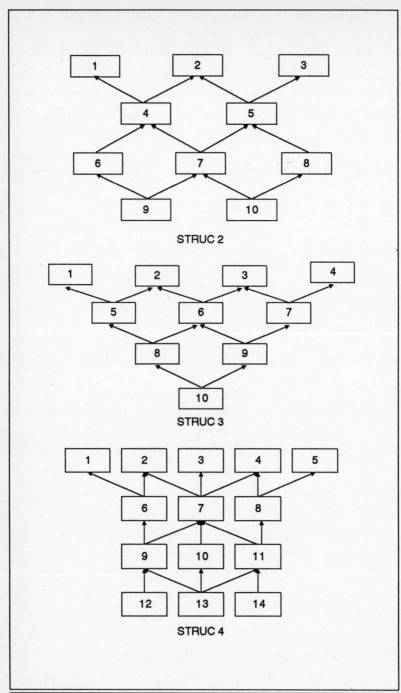

Figure 6.2. Three product structures.

$$S_i = 0.5 \times \tilde{h}_i \times \overline{D}_i \times (TBO)^2 \tag{6.9}$$

where TBO_i is the Time Between Ordering for item i, which is based
on the EOQ-formula derived for single level problems with constant
average (in)dependent demand of $\overline{D}_i$. The TBO is consequently only a
rough estimate of the true time between ordering in a multilevel production planning problem. Experiments were carried out for each problem
with TBO's equal to 2, 3 and 4 periods. All time-dependent production
costs $p_{i,t}$ are set equal to zero. For each product structure-TBO combination 10 different problem instances are generated, in total resulting
in 120 instances per set. Problems belonging to Set I are handled by
$\overline{MLLPH}$, while problems belonging to set II are handled by $MLLPH$,
since non-zero demand occurs for components[1]. The maximum number
of iterations (I^{max}) is set equal to 500 for both heuristic procedures,
and the procedures stop when the gap $\Delta Z = 100\% \times (UB - LB)/LB$
becomes smaller than $\epsilon = 0.005$ or the maximum number of iterations
is reached, whichever occurs first.

Table 6.1. Computational results for MLLPH.

		Problem set I			Problem set II		
product structure	*TBO*	ΔZ	O	$\overline{CPU}$	ΔZ	O	$\overline{CPU}$
	2	0.00	9	14.89	3.26	0	99.59
STRUC1	3	0.00	9	13.64	2.59	0	90.78
	4	0.00	8	21.97	6.32	0	82.80
	2	0.02	1	131.13	12.63	0	150.25
STRUC2	3	1.11	4	113.38	7.61	0	143.95
	4	0.04	5	126.01	10.04	0	138.00
	2	0.00	9	58.35	5.90	0	157.98
STRUC3	3	0.00	10	51.19	12.51	0	130.12
	4	0.00	4	104.72	8.95	0	124.36
	2	3.17	3	193.58	17.62	0	207.51
STRUC4	3	1.99	6	145.21	15.58	0	228.16
	4	2.43	0	201.20	5.47	0	217.20

Computational results are shown in Table 6.1. Here, $\overline{\Delta Z}$ (columns

---

[1]Unfortunately, lacking details and the code of the heuristic proposed in [2], we
were not able to run our heuristic and that of [2] on the same data.

3 and 6) denotes the *average* gap, O (columns 4 and 7) denotes the number of problems solved to *proven* optimality ($\Delta Z = 0$) and $\overline{CPU}$ (columns 5 and 8) is the average CPU-time, expressed in seconds.

From the experiments we conclude that the "Lagrangean" lower bounds obtained by $\overline{MLLP}$ are rather tight and that the upper bounding heuristic seems to perform adequately, although both the gap and the required CPU-time increase when the problem-size increases and/or when the complexity of the product structure grows. On the other hand, the time between ordering (TBO) seems to influence the quality of the solutions and the required CPU-time only slightly.

Heuristic $MLLPH$ appears to be less effective than $\overline{MLLPH}$, which is demonstrated by the differences in total average gap (computed over all 120 test problems) which amounts to 1.23 % for Set I versus 9.04 % for Set II. Furthermore, large differences exist in required total average CPU-time (again, computed over all 120 instances), which increases from 98.69 seconds for Set I to 147.55 seconds for Set II. Moreover, $MLLPH$ seems to be unable to prove optimality for one single problem instance; the total number of problems solved to proven optimality decreases from 68 (about 60 %) for Set I to zero for Set II.

The differences in performance between the two heuristics are mainly caused by the fact that $\overline{MLLPH}$ takes into account an obviously important property of the optimal solution (i.e. the nesting property). Taking into account this property (in a "Lagrangean" way) leads to more meaningful values for all Lagrangean multipliers involved, and consequently improves the quality of the lower bounds significantly. Since good values of these multipliers also influence the quality of the "Lagrangean" upper bounding heuristic, the convergence speed of the subgradient optimization procedure is also substantially improved. This explains the difference in quality of the solutions and computational requirements between $MLLPH$ and its adapted version $\overline{MLLPH}$.

6.4 Summary and discussion

In this chapter we consider the Multilevel Lotsizing Problem (MLLP). After an overview of previous research on MLLP, which shows that the problem for specific product structures, like e.g. assembly systems, has been studied extensively by a large number of authors, we introduce a new heuristic for the *general* MLLP with independent demand for all items. As far as we know, for this particular problem no other procedures have been proposed and tested by other authors until now.

Similar to the heuristic developed by Afentakis and Gavish [2] for the restricted problem with demand for end-items only, in our heuristic lower bounds are obtained by Lagrangean relaxation of the non-negativity constraint on inventory. By doing so, the MLLP decomposes into single-item subproblems which are solved by a fast dynamic programming algorithm (e.g. Wagner-Whitin). Our heuristic differs from the method presented in [2] in the "Lagrangean" way in which the nesting property is used to tighten lower bounds, and in the simple and effective way upper bounds are obtained, using a "Lagrangean" cost-adaptation heuristic which can be seen as a generalization of Blackburn and Millen's [18] single-pass heuristic for assembly problems.

Computational results on a set of 240 test problems show that our heuristic is rather effective for problems with independent demand for end-items only, but for more general problems with independent demand for all items we conclude that the performance may decrease substantially, both in terms of quality of the solutions as well as in terms of required CPU-time.

Finally, an important conclusion of the study reported here is that general MLLP's are, at least heuristically, *considerably harder* to handle than MLLP's with demand for end-items only.

Future research on MLLP will focus on the embedding of our heuristics in a branch-and-bound procedure.

Chapter 7

The Capacitated Problem

7.1 Introduction

In this chapter the multilevel capacitated lotsizing problem (MLCLP) is considered. This problem, which was originally stated by Billington et al. [16] in 1983, occurs when production schedules have to be determined for multilevel production-inventory systems in the presence of capacity constraints on production facilities. It is assumed that time-phased demand is dynamic and deterministic, while backlogging is not allowed. The objective is to determine a time-phased production schedule for end items as well as for components, such that the sum of item-dependent setup costs and item-dependent inventory holding costs is minimized, while period-dependent capacity limitations must not be violated. The problems studied in this chapter are restricted in that neither setup times nor overtime work are considered. Furthermore, as in a second paper by Billington [15], it is assumed that only one bottleneck exists, which is situated at a single level in the product structure. MLCLP which satisfy the restrictions made above can be formulated as the following mixed integer-linear program:

MLCLP:

$$Z_{MLCLP} = \min \sum_{i=1}^{N} \sum_{t=1}^{T} (S_i y_{i,t} + h_i I_{i,t} + p_{i,t} x_{i,t}) \tag{7.1}$$

subject to

$$I_{i,t-1} + x_{i,t} - d_{i,t} - \sum_{j \in S_i} g_{i,j} x_{j,t} = I_{i,t} \qquad i = 1, ..., N; \, t = 1, ..., T \quad (7.2)$$

$$\sum_{i \in C} b_i x_{i,t} \leq C_t \qquad\qquad\qquad\qquad t = 1, .., T \tag{7.3}$$

$$x_{i,t} \leq M y_{i,t} \qquad\qquad\qquad\qquad i = 1, .., N; \, t = 1, .., T \quad (7.4)$$

$$x_{i,t} \geq 0 \qquad\qquad\qquad\qquad\quad i = 1, .., N; \, t = 1, .., T \quad (7.5)$$

$$I_{i,t} \geq 0 \qquad\qquad\qquad\qquad\quad i = 1, .., N; \, t = 1, .., T \quad (7.6)$$

$$y_{i,t} \in \{0, 1\} \qquad\qquad\qquad\quad i = 1, .., N; \, t = 1, ..T \quad (7.7)$$

The parameters in the model are the same as defined in Section 6.1. In addition, we define C as the set of items at the capacitated level and b_i as the capacity absorbtion coefficient for item i. Furthermore, C_t is the number of capacity units available at the capacitated level in period t.

The objective, to minimize the sum of setup and holding costs, is represented by equation (7.1). Equations (7.2) are balance equations which state that dependent and independent demand are fulfilled either from inventory or from production in the current period. (Analogous to Chapter 6, we assume, without loss of generality, the leadtimes to be zero.) The inequalities (7.3) enforce that production (in each period) be within the limitations set by available capacity. The coupling constraints (7.4) together with (7.7) state that production for item i in period t is possible only if the setup variable for item i in period t is set equal to one. Finally, inequalities (7.5) require production quantities to be nonnegative while (7.6) assure that backlogging is not allowed.

Note: When referring to a *feasible production schedule* for MLCLP a set of variables $x = \{x_{i,t}\}$ *all i,t* and $I = \{I_{i,t}\}$ *all i,t* satisfying equations (7.2),..,(7.7) is meant. The corresponding set of variables $y = \{y_{i,t}\}$ is called a *feasible setup pattern*. A feasible production schedule, (x, I), of MLCLP is called *optimal* if it minimizes Z_{MLCLP} as defined in (7.1).

A number of solution procedures have been proposed for MLCLP. Billington et al. [15] propose a branch and bound algorithm for solving MLCLP with a single bottle-neck facility, using Lagrangean relaxations to generate lower bounds. Upper bounds are obtained using simple smoothing heuristics. Reported tests with the algorithm show that computation times grow rapidly with the size of the problem. Recently, Lozano et al. [77] proposed a primal-dual solution procedure for solving the multilevel capacitated lotsizing problem (which also includes setup times). However, only limited results for small test problems were reported. For special product structures, like assembly systems, another modelling approach can be taken. This approach is based on the so-called "facility location" formulation of the multilevel uncapacitated lotsizing problem. In Section 7.2 an extension of this model to capacitated problems, as proposed by Maes et al. [80], will be given. For serial systems, which are in turn special cases of assembly systems, some well-known single level heuristics, like Dixon and Silver, can be adapted to handle the multilevel situation. These algorithms are discussed in Billington et al. [14]. For a more extensive overview of multilevel capacitated lotsizing research prior to 1987 the reader is referred to Bahl et al. [8].

Three basic heuristic techniques for solving MLCLP are compared in this chapter. One is based on LP relaxation while the other two are based on heuristic search techniques. The three heuristics are:

- *Simulated Annealing (statistical cooling)*. Here the solution set is systematically, but stochastically, searched for a good solution. This method is an extension of the procedure followed by Kuik and Salomon [69] to solve the multilevel uncapacitated problem.

- *Tabu Search.* In this approach the solution set is searched quickly, as in simulated annealing, in a (restricted) greedy fashion while keeping log of, and updating a prohibited, tabu, subset of solutions.

- *LP-Based Heuristics.* In this approach the LP relaxations of a reformulation of MLCLP is considered. Two of these heuristics are purely based on rounding LP solutions, while two other heuristics combine LP with elements from simulated annealing and tabu search.

Details of the three approaches are given in Section 7.2. Section 7.3 describes the experimental design and presents computational results. Finally, in Section 7.4, some conclusions are drawn.

7.2 Three new heuristics

This section subsequently discusses a heuristic based on simulated annealing, a tabu search heuristic, and finally a number of LP-based heuristics.

7.2.1 Searching with simulated annealing

The class of heuristics presented here uses simulated annealing (SA) to solve MLCLP. SA has recently been applied to difficult combinatorial optimization problems. Examples can be found in Aarts and van Laarhoven [1], who describe SA algorithms for the travelling salesman problem and for several job scheduling problems. An application of SA to uncapacitated multilevel lotsizing is given in [69]. Here this algorithm is extended to MLCLP. In essence, SA is a very simple nondeterministic optimization technique which constructs a sequence of solutions (*a walk or path*), through the set of permissible solutions called the *state space*. The procedure for deciding which solution to step to next is called *transition mechanism*. This transition mechanism requires as input the current solution, and some extra input specific to the SA implementation at hand. This extra input concerns information on the set of potential solutions reachable from the current solution, called the *neighbourhood* of the current solution, the determination of the *likelihood* of considering each neighbour and the setting of an *acceptance probability* for the selected neighbour. Usually, for minimization problems, after selecting a candidate neighbour (by invoking the transition mechanism) and determining a likelihood p from a $U(0, 1)$ distribution, the acceptance probability (p^{accept}) is computed as,

$$p^{accept} = \begin{cases} \exp[-\beta(Z^{nb} - Z^{cs})] & \text{if } Z^{nb} > Z^{cs} \\ \\ 1 & \text{otherwise} \end{cases}$$

where Z^{nb} is the value of the objective function at the candidate neighbour solution and Z^{cs} is the value of the objective function at the current solution.

The walk proceeds to the candidate neighbour when $p \leq p^{accept}$. Otherwise, the neighbour is rejected and the transition mechanism is invoked again.

A subwalk during which the parameter β is held constant, is called *a chain* and the chain length is denoted by L. The *control parameter β* is nonnegative and increases after every L steps of the walk. Although many variants for updating β have been proposed, β is updated according to,

$$\beta := \beta/\alpha \text{ with } 0 < \alpha < 1.$$

The newly introduced constant α is called the *descending parameter*. Finally one has -in addition to the transition mechanism- to specify a *stopping criterion*. Here many variants have also been proposed, but in this heuristic the number of chains to be evaluated is chosen as stopping criterion. For more (theoretical) details on SA the reader is referred to van Laarhoven [71], and the review by Glover and Greenberg, [49].

As a first point specific to the implementation of SA to MLCLP the state-space definition is mentioned. This space is chosen as the set of feasible setup patterns $y = \{y_{i,t}\}$. The walk through the state space starts at the initial setup pattern y, for which $y_{i,t} = 1$ for all $i = 1, .., N$ and $t = 1, .., T$. The corresponding optimal value of the objective function $(Z_P(y))$ can be computed by solving the following linear program:

P :

$$Z_P(y) = \min \sum_{i=1}^{N} \sum_{t=1}^{T} h_i I_{i,t} + C$$

subject to

(7.2), (7.3), (7.5), (7.6)

where C is a constant term equal to $\sum_{i=1}^{N} \sum_{t=1}^{T} S_i y_{i,t}$.

This problem was studied by McClain et al. in [86]. For the special case with *one bottle-neck at a single level in the product structure*, they suggest a *greedy algorithm* which solves P optimally:

Greedy Algorithm:

Step 1:   Start at the lowest numbered level in the product structure, not yet considered. If this level is uncapacitated, goto step 2, otherwise, goto Step 3. If all levels in the product structure have been considered, then *STOP*.

Step 2   Plan production for each item i at the current level *lot-for-lot*, i.e. set the production $x_{i,t}$ equal to $d_{i,t} + \sum_{j<i} g_{i,j} x_{j,t}$ in each period t. Goto Step 1.

Step 3: Plan production at the capacitated level in the following way: Select the unplanned item with the highest holding cost per unit. Plan demand for this item as late as possible. Update available capacity and proceed until all items at this level have been planned. Goto Step 1. (See also Appendix B of Chapter 3.)

In this heuristic it is necessary to compute the value of the objective function for *arbitrary* setup patterns. However, for arbitrary setup patterns y, the conditions

$$x_{i,t} \leq M y_{i,t} \quad \text{for } i = 1, .., N; \, t = 1, .., T.$$

must be added to P.

As far as we know, no efficient solution procedure for solving this extended problem is available, other than a LP-based algorithm suggested by McClain et al. [86]. This algorithm, which uses Dantzig-Wolfe decomposition, is shown to require less computation time than straightforward application of the simplex method, but it is still too time consuming to be used repeatedly in a simulated annealing algorithm. For this reason we chose to use an algorithm, based on the greedy algorithm discussed above, to find an approximation, $Z_P^A(y)$ to $Z_P(y)$.

First, note that for arbitrary setup patterns lot-for-lot production at the uncapacitated levels may no longer be possible. Second, observe that there exists an optimal solution to MLCLP, in which at the *uncapacitated levels* production for item i in period t *only* takes place when inventory is zero at the end of period $t - 1$, that is:

$$I_{i,t-1} x_{i,t} = 0 \text{ for } i \notin C$$

The proof of this property, which is called the *Zero-Inventory Property*, can be found in the Appendix at the end of this chapter.

Using these observations, the following *modified* greedy algorithm is used:

Modified Greedy Algorithm

Step 1:   Start at the lowest numbered level in the product structure, not yet considered. If this level is uncapacitated,
goto step 2, otherwise, goto Step 3. If all levels in the
product structure have been considered, then *STOP*.

Step 2:   Plan production for each item i at the current level using the Zero-Inventory Property thereby ensuring that
whenever a setup is made the production quantity is
large enough to cover demand in all subsequent periods
in which there is no setup. Thus, if t_1 is the first period for which $y_{i,t} = 1$ and t_2 the next period for which
$y_{i,t} = 1$, then set x_{i,t_1} equal to $\sum_{t=t_1}^{t_2-1}[d_{i,t} + \sum_{j<i} g_{i,j} x_{j,t}]$
and set $x_{i,t}$ equal to zero for $t = t_1+1, .., t_2-1$. Proceed
in this way until the end of the planning horizon.

Step 3:   Plan production at the capacitated level in the following
way: Select the unplanned item with the highest holding
cost per unit. Plan demand for this item as late as
possible, thereby putting the production quantity $x_{i,t}$
equal to zero when $y_{i,t}$ equals zero. Update available
capacity and proceed until all items at this level have
been planned. If the production plan becomes *infeasible*
then *STOP* $(p^{accept} = 0)$, otherwise goto Step 1.

The Modified Greedy Algorithm does not necessarily yield an optimal
solution due to the occurrence of zero-valued setup variables in some
item-period combinations. The zero-valued setup variables prevent production in these periods and therefore, corroborating the capacity constraint already present, effectively act as capacity restrictions active at
multiple levels.
Thus, the value $Z_P^A(y)$ obtained by the Modified Greedy Algorithm is
only an approximation for the true optimum $Z_P(y)$. It can be obtained
quickly and can therefore be used repeatedly in a simulated annealing
algorithm. This is, however, at the expense of guarantied convergence

of the SA algorithm to an optimal solution with probability one (in the long run).

When the stopping criterion is reached, $Z_P(\bar{y})$ is computed, where $\bar{y}$ is the setup pattern which yielded the smallest value of $Z_P^A(y)$ during the course of the SA algorithm.

A second point specific to the implementation of the SA algorithm is the specification of the transition mechanism. Based on experiences with the uncapacitated multilevel lotsizing problem (see [69])), we chose to test the following transition mechanism structure:

TM: Given a setup pattern y, which is feasible with respect to restrictions (7.2),..,(7.7), a setup pattern y' is a neighbour of y if it is feasible and if

$$\sum_{i=1}^{N}\sum_{t=1}^{T}|y_{i,t} - y'_{i,t}| = 1$$

The neighbourhood structure defines our transition mechanism, which can be summarized as follows: Select randomly an item number i^* (from an $U(1, N)$ distribution), and a period number t^* (from an $U(1, T)$ distribution), and invert the corresponding setup variable, i.e. $y_{i^*,t^*} = 1 - y_{i^*,t^*}$. Repeat this procedure until a feasible setup pattern is found.

Another implementation of the SA heuristic (in combination with Linear Programming) is discussed in Section 7.2.3.

7.2.2   Searching with a tabu list

Tabu search (TS) is a method which has recently drawn attention as an alternative to SA for solving difficult combinatorial optimization problems. Glover [48] describes an implementation for solving general mixed integer linear programs, and Hertz and de Werra [61,109] describe applications to node colouring in a graph, scheduling, character recognition, etc.

The TS method for solving MLCLP proceeds in a spirit analogous to SA in that it also involves a walk through the state space of feasible production schedules as defined by the feasible setup patterns. The walk is constructed one step at a time. Suppose it has come to setup pattern y. Then, from the set of neighbours, a subset containing k neighbours that are not in a tabu list (to be described below) are randomly generated using transition mechanism TM and placed in a solution list, $\mathcal{L}_k$. The new setup pattern, y' is determined as:

$$y' = \min\{y \in \mathcal{L}_k \mid Z_{LP}^A(y) \text{ is minimal}\}$$

were Z_{LP}^A is obtained by using the Extended Greedy Algorithm. Note that although y' leads to the best solution in $\mathcal{L}_k$, it is not necessarily better than the current solution y.

The role of the tabu list $\mathcal{T}_m$, which contains the m most recently visited setup patterns, is to avoid cycling in the state space (to a certain extent, since a cycle, longer than the number of solutions in the tabu list, cannot be excluded beforehand).

Finally, as for the SA algorithm, TS starts with $y_{i,t} = 1$ for all $i = 1, .., N$ and $t = 1, .., T$ and stops after a prespecified number of feasible setup patterns have been evaluated. An alternative implementation of TS (in combination with Linear Programming) is discussed in the next section.

7.2.3   Linear programming based heuristics for assembly systems

LP-relaxation and subsequent rounding to obtain an all integer solution is one of the first ideas that comes to mind when considering MLCLP. However, direct application of such a method leads to poor results, due to the large integrality gap of the LP-relaxation. As noted by Rosling [92], the integrality gap for the uncapacitated problem can be reduced by reformulating MLCLP as a facility location problem. Unfortunately, this reformulation applies only to assembly product structures. Below, the facility location formulation is extended to *capacitated* assembly systems. The Extended Facility Location Problem (EFLP) can be formulated as:

EFLP:

$$Z_{EFLP} = \min \sum_{i=1}^{N} \left(\sum_{\tau=1}^{T} \sum_{t=\tau}^{T} (t-\tau) d_{e_i,t} \tilde{h}_i p_{i,\tau,t} + \sum_{\tau=1}^{T} S_i y_{i,\tau} \right) \qquad (7.8)$$

subject to

$$\sum_{\tau=1}^{t} p_{i,\tau,t} = 1 \qquad\qquad i = 1, .., N; \ t = 1, .., T \qquad\qquad (7.9)$$

$$p_{i,\tau,t} \leq y_{i,\tau} \qquad\qquad i = 1, .., N; \ \tau = 1, .., t; \ t = 1, .., T \qquad (7.10)$$

$$\sum_{u=1}^{\tau} p_{i,u,t} \geq \sum_{u=1}^{\tau} p_{\mathcal{S}_i,u,t} \qquad i = 1, .., N; \ \tau = 1, .., t; \ t = 1, .., T \qquad (7.11)$$

$$\sum_{i \in \mathcal{C}} \sum_{t=\tau}^{T} b_i d_{e_i,t} p_{i,\tau,t} \leq C_\tau \quad \tau = 1, .., T \qquad\qquad (7.12)$$

$$p_{i,\tau,t} \geq 0 \qquad\qquad i = 1, .., N; \ \tau = 1, .., T; \ t = \tau, .., T \quad (7.13)$$

$$y_{i,t} \geq 0 \qquad\qquad i = 1, .., N; \ t = 1, .., T \qquad\qquad (7.14)$$

where:

$\tilde{h}_i \quad = \quad$ the "echelon" holding cost, which equals $(h_i - \sum_{j \in \mathcal{P}_i} h_j)$. In what follows it is assumed that these costs are *non-negative*.

e_i =   the unique end item of which i is a predecessor.

$p_{i,\tau,t}$ =   the fraction of demand for item e_i in period t, produced for item i in period τ.

Other variables and parameters are as defined before.

The objective is represented by equation (7.8), whereby Z_{EFLP} is the cost of an optimal production schedule. The set of equations (7.9) state that the fractional productions add up to one, thereby ensuring that demand is completely satisfied. Inequalities (7.10), together with (7.14), imply that whenever production for item i occurs in period t, the corresponding setup variable, $y_{i,t}$, is equal to 1. Inequalities (7.11) state that sufficient components are available when starting production for item i in period t. Inequalities (7.12) express that production complies with bounds set by capacity, while (7.13) state that production quantities are nonnegative. It must be noted that this model formulation is completely stated in terms of production and setup variables. Inventory variables have been eliminated. Note also that gozinto factors, defined implicitly in EFLP, are equal to zero or one. For assembly problems this composes no loss in generality since any assembly problem can be transformed into an equivalent assembly problem with gozinto factors equal to zero or one. Furthermore, in the model formulation for EFLP it is implicitly assumed that demand $d_{i,t}$ is nonzero for end items only.

By an immediate transformation problem EFLP can be seen to be equivalent, for assembly structures, to MLCLP. Any solution $\{x_{i,t}, y_{i,t}\}$ to MLCLP can be associated with a solution $\{p_{i,\tau,t}, y_{i,t}\}$ of EFLP by the obvious identification of setup variables and by determining the production variables $\{x_{i,\tau}\}$ as:

$$x_{i,\tau} = \sum_{t=\tau}^{T} p_{i,\tau,t} d_{e_i,t}$$

(The reader will have no difficulty establishing an inverse transformation constructing a solution to EFLP from a solution to MLCLP.) Furthermore, under this transformation, the values of the objective functions of the problems remain unaltered.

In addition to the set of inequalities (7.8) to (7.14) a set of valid inequalities based on available capacity can be derived to improve the LP-relaxation of EFLP (see Maes et al. [80]).

In [80] a number of heuristics based on *rounding* (noninteger) solutions of the LP-relaxation of EFLP are proposed and tested. The heuristics have the common feature that in each step one or more setup variables, $y_{i,t}$, are selected from the set of free setup variables and fixed to either zero or one. The LP, resulting from substitution of the fixed variables, is then solved again. Sometimes, backtracking steps are involved (multi-pass heuristics). The heuristics differ in the way the variables, to be fixed in an iteration step, are chosen. It was decided to use two fixing strategies in the experiments, as a bench mark against which the simulated annealing and tabu search heuristics are tested. The Linear Programming Rounding Strategies that will be considered are a single pass heuristic ($LPRS_1$) and a multi-pass heuristic ($LPRS_2$). For a more detailed description of the heuristics, the reader is referred to [80].

Besides the (deterministic) fixing strategies, two other heuristics are tested that combine Linear Programming with Simulated Annealing and with Tabu Search, respectively:

LPSA: First, solve the LP-relaxation of $EFLP$ (LP_{EFLP}) and fix all integer setup variables in this solution at their respective values. The item-period combinations with non-integer setup variables form the set $\mathcal{F}$, or:

$$\mathcal{F} = \{(i,t) \mid \epsilon \leq y_{i,t} \leq 1 - \epsilon \text{ in } LP_{EFLP}.\}$$

where $\epsilon = 0.001$. The setup variables $y_{i,t}$ for which $(i,t) \in \mathcal{F}$ are initialized to 1. The simulated annealing algorithm starts from this initial configuration and uses the transition mechanism to obtain a new setup pattern, thereby only changing the value of setup variables $y_{i,t}$ for which $(i,t) \in \mathcal{F}$. The algorithm is further identical to the simulated annealing algorithm presented in Section 7.2.1.

LPTS: This algorithm is identical to LPSA, as far as the starting solution and the transition mechanism are concerned. However, instead of a simulated annealing algorithm a tabu search algorithm (as described in Section
7.2.2) is used to generate production schedules.

It was decided to test algorithms that combine LP with statistical
search methods for two reasons. First, a good starting solution, which
is hopefully generated by the LP-relaxation of EFLP, may prove to be
useful in obtaining good quality solutions in relatively short computation time. Second, by preventing the algorithm from changing setup
variables not in the set $\mathcal{F}$, the state space is kept (much) smaller. This
will hopefully restrict the search to a subset of the state space which
contains "good" solutions. However, like in partial branch and bound
algorithms, no guarantee can be given for the latter statement.

7.3   Computational results

The SA, TS and LP heuristics have been tested on a large number
of problems with different parameter settings. In this chapter a rep-
resentative summary of these experiments is given. The test problems
considered here are obtained from two different product structures, subsequently denoted by STRUC1 and STRUC2 (Figure 7.1).

STRUC1 and STRUC2 are twelve period planning problems ($T = 12$)
with six ($N = 6$) and seven ($N = 7$) items respectively. All nonzero
gozinto factors ($g_{i,j}$) are assumed to be equal to one. Both product
structures have three levels and the middle level is capacitated (capacity absorption coefficients are equal to one).
Demand for end items in each period is generated from a normal distribution with a mean of 20 and a standard deviation of 5 (independent
demand for the other items is zero). Echelon holding costs for each
item are generated from the uniform distribution [0.3,0.5]. Setup costs
are computed according to formula (6.9), where TBO was varied over
2,3 and 4 periods. Finally, the capacity utilization, ρ, defined as the
total requirement (in production time) divided by total available ca-

pacity at the capacitated level, is set to 0.6, 0.8 and 0.9 respectively. Summarizing, the experimental design consists of problems with 2 different product structures, 3 different TBO's and 3 different capacity utilizations, resulting in a total of $2 \times 3 \times 3 = 18$ problems.

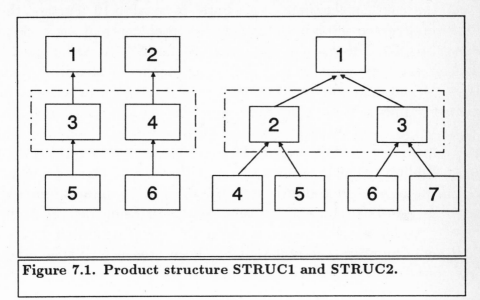

Figure 7.1. Product structure STRUC1 and STRUC2.

One is forced to compare the quality of the heuristics with lower bounds instead of optimal solutions, since it is hardly possible to obtain (proven) optimal solutions by standard branch and bound algorithms (like the software package MPSX), even for small problems with as little as 4 items and 6 planning periods. Also, no optimal solutions obtained by special purpose algorithms for standard sets of test problems are known to us.

Although the SA and the TS algorithm are applicable to general product structures, experiments were limited to series (STRUC1) and assembly (STRUC2) product structures for two reasons mainly. The first reason is that reasonable lower bounds can be computed (using the LP-relaxation of $EFLP$) for these types of product structures only. The second reason for the limitation is that the LP-based heuristics are applicable to assembly systems only.

Based on experiences with different parameter settings (see also [69])

the following parameters are selected for the SA and LPSA-heuristics:
The chain length L is set equal to 50, the descending parameter α is set
equal to 0.95 and the maximum number of chains to be evaluated is set
equal to 100. For the TS and LPTS heuristic the length of the solution
list and the length of the tabu list are both set equal to 10. Further, the
number of accepted setup patterns, i.e., the total length of the walk, is
set equal to 500. For this parameter setting the CPU-times for the TS
algorithm are comparable to the CPU-times for the SA algorithms (see
Tables 7.1 and 7.2). For the SA and TS heuristics each experiment is
repeated 5 times with different random seeds.

The LP heuristics were programmed in FORTRAN and integrated with
the XMP-library which contains LP algorithms. The SA and the TS
heuristics were also programmed in FORTRAN. All programs were run
on a SUN 3-workstation with math co-processor using the f77 FOR-
TRAN compiler which is available under the operating system UNIX.
The random number generator that has been used is available in the
library of the f77-compiler.

Computational results obtained with SA, TS and the linear programming based heuristics $LPRS_1$, $LPRS_2$, LPSA and LPTS are shown in
Table 7.1 (for STRUC1) and in Table 7.2 (for STRUC2). The first
two columns in these tables denote the time between ordering (TBO)
and the capacity utilisation (ρ) respectively. The (average) quality of
the heuristics ($Q_{average}$), which is shown in columns three to seven, is
computed as:

$$Q_{average} = \frac{\text{Average solution obtained by heuristic}}{Z_{LP(EFLP)}}$$

where $Z_{LP(EFLP)}$ is the lower bound obtained by solving the LP-relaxation
of EFLP. Note that for the heuristics SA, TS, LPSA and LPTS the average is computed over five runs.

The CPU-time required to solve the LP-relaxation of EFLP is shown in
column eight (LP_{EFLP}), and the (average) CPU-time for the heuristics
is displayed in columns nine to thirteen. All CPU-times are in seconds.

TBO	ρ	$Q_{average}$ LPRS$_1$ / LPRS$_2$	SA	TS	LPSA	LPTS	CPU-Time (seconds) LP_{EFLP}	LPRS$_1$ / LPRS$_2$	SA	TS	LPSA	LPTS
2	0.6	1.13	1.03	1.03	1.03	1.03	239.97	141.50	82.41	84.91	123.71	144.03
		1.03	(0.02)	(0.01)	(0.00)	(0.00)		593.54	(1.09)	(3.38)	(1.12)	(1.96)
	0.8	1.07	1.08	1.08	1.07	1.06	187.91	121.06	96.69	102.73	123.05	127.58
		1.06	(0.02)	(0.02)	(0.01)	(0.01)		604.04	(0.90)	(6.16)	(1.34)	(1.97)
	0.9	1.05	1.07	1.08	1.06	1.08	183.73	109.41	109.54	119.65	124.70	133.21
		1.04	(0.02)	(0.03)	(0.00)	(0.04)		530.98	(2.17)	(2.09)	(0.97)	(8.47)
3	0.6	1.13	1.07	1.08	1.02	1.02	391.16	214.78	86.64	93.01	114.07	121.72
		1.03	(0.03)	(0.05)	(0.00)	(0.00)		1081.32	(0.77)	(4.09)	(2.02)	(2.22)
	0.8	1.29	1.13	1.17	1.15	1.16	455.69	604.73	101.05	109.18	151.34	162.11
		1.18	(0.01)	(0.02)	(0.00)	(0.00)		2275.68	(0.49)	(2.60)	(2.41)	(4.30)
	0.9	1.19	1.18	1.19	1.17	1.21	361.78	272.89	115.19	125.57	128.14	137.68
		1.17	(0.02)	(0.02)	(0.01)	(0.01)		1261.78	(1.09)	(2.40)	(2.12)	(4.30)
4	0.6	1.26	1.13	1.14	1.16	1.17	756.59	506.80	89.77	94.33	152.62	177.09
		1.11	(0.02)	(0.04)	(0.00)	(0.00)		3000.90	(0.83)	(2.74)	(2.31)	(4.40)
	0.8	1.23	1.22	1.21	1.20	1.21	872.16	451.70	103.85	109.10	165.83	177.51
		1.32	(0.02)	(0.03)	(0.00)	(0.02)		2466.36	(1.06)	(2.21)	(5.21)	(5.13)
	0.9	1.21	1.21	1.27	1.19	1.25	421.59	316.14	115.87	130.88	146.41	156.38
		1.22	(0.04)	(0.02)	(0.05)	(0.03)		1339.48	(2.59)	(1.96)	(4.71)	(5.05)

Table 7.1. Computational results for STRUC1.

TBO	ρ	$Q_{average}$ $LPRS_1$ / $LPRS_2$	SA	TS	LPSA	LPTS	CPU-Time (seconds) LP_{EFLP}	$LPRS_1$ / $LPRS_2$	SA	TS	LPSA	LPTS
2	0.6	1.31 / 1.21	1.15 (0.02)	1.17 (0.04)	1.14 (0.03)	1.16 (0.02)	563.90	666.62 / 979.14	82.46 (0.51)	91.52 (3.93)	97.48 (1.67)	114.11 (5.47)
	0.8	1.35 / 1.31	1.08 (0.02)	1.10 (0.04)	1.25 (0.02)	1.28 (0.01)	475.56	378.32 / 1686.36	82.46 (0.51)	91.52 (3.93)	118.54 (1.93)	127.95 (8.53)
	0.9	1.49 / 1.38	1.24 (0.03)	1.22 (0.04)	1.24 (0.02)	1.26 (0.02)	333.98	555.16 / 911.90	94.47 (1.72)	109.97 (6.64)	107.04 (1.04)	129.50 (7.12)
3	0.6	1.42 / 1.45	1.22 (0.03)	1.23 (0.06)	1.31 (0.00)	1.31 (0.00)	2501.78	1266.62 / 3276.08	82.60 (0.69)	92.28 (2.67)	175.02 (1.05)	215.82 (2.97)
	0.8	1.48 / 1.41	1.30 (0.06)	1.28 (0.04)	1.34 (0.01)	1.36 (0.06)	654.30	685.16 / 3730.72	92.07 (2.36)	103.23 (2.47)	142.69 (1.35)	172.41 (13.30)
	0.9	1.50 / 1.44	1.27 (0.05)	1.31 (0.04)	1.28 (0.01)	1.27 (0.08)	693.68	839.96 / 954.16	98.21 (2.20)	114.73 (4.19)	116.54 (2.33)	133.45 (8.73)
4	0.6	1.60 / 1.58	1.29 (0.02)	1.32 (0.06)	1.32 (0.04)	1.34 (0.05)	1395.86	2122.18 / 4289.50	84.26 (0.81)	89.22 (2.33)	145.65 (11.56)	189.24 (17.75)
	0.8	1.38 / 1.39	1.30 (0.02)	1.27 (0.06)	1.37 (0.01)	1.39 (0.07)	908.48	555.60 / 2962.32	92.86 (2.44)	102.86 (3.30)	177.21 (3.20)	221.20 (25.87)
	0.9	1.39 / 1.48	1.25 (0.07)	1.22 (0.06)	1.25 (0.01)	1.27 (0.05)	324.34	418.88 / 940.54	99.12 (1.20)	109.22 (3.03)	145.34 (1.59)	155.06 (8.78)

Table 7.2. Computational results for STRUC2.

Standard deviations for $Q_{average}$ and for the required CPU-time are presented (in brackets) for the stochastic search heuristics SA, TS, LPSA and LPTS. It must be noted that the time required for the LP-heuristics LPRS$_1$, LPRS$_2$, LPSA and LPTS is *exclusive* of the time required to solve LP_{EFLP}.

From the experiments it is concluded that the computation time for the initial LP lower bound heavily depends on the complexity of the problem structure (e.g. problem size, type of product structure, etc), since the computation times for LP_{EFLP} for STRUC1 and the more complex structure STRUC2 are largely different. It can also be seen that computation time decreases as the capacity utilisation ρ increases. This is due to the fact that for high capacity utilisation the number of feasible production schedules to be considered by the simplex algorithm is much smaller than for low capacitated problems. From the observation made by Rosling [92] that the LP-relaxation of EFLP yields an all-integer solution for uncapacitated problems very often, one would expect lower bounds to be better (and the number of fractional variables smaller) for low-capacitated problems. It seems however that even for low-capacitated problems a large number of setup variables are fractional, and therefore many setup variables must be rounded, which results in large computation times for the heuristics LPRS$_1$ and LPRS$_2$.

For STRUC1, a comparison of the results obtained by LPRS$_1$ and LPRS$_2$ with SA and TS shows that the differences in $Q_{average}$ are especially noticeable for lower capacitated problems. For these problems, SA and TS outperform LPRS$_1$ by at least 5%, but the difference sometimes increases up to 13%. The multi-pass heuristic LPRS$_2$ outperforms the single pass heuristic LPRS$_1$ and performs in some cases a few percent better than SA and TS. However, the required CPU-time is for LPRS$_1$ between 2 and 12 times higher and for LPRS$_2$ between 6 and 30 times higher than for SA and TS. The difference between SA and TS is very small, both with respect to $Q_{average}$ and CPU-time. Furthermore, the combined heuristics LPSA and LPTS do not seem to perform much better than SA and TS, except perhaps for some low-capacitated problems with TBO=3. Finally, it must be noted that the SA, TS, LPSA and LPTS implementations require larger computation times when capacity utilisation becomes higher, due to the fact that many infeasible setup patterns will have to be rejected.

For STRUC2, SA and TS perform at least 10 % better than $LPRS_1$. The difference in $Q_{average}$ between the single pass heuristic and the multi-pass heuristic ranges in between 9% in favour of the single pass heuristic, up to 11% in favour of the multi-pass heuristic. Moreover, CPU-times for LP_{EFLP}, $LPRS_1$ and $LPRS_2$ increase dramatically, to about 40 times the CPU-time required for SA and TS. It is observed, in accordance with the results obtained for STRUC1, that for STRUC2 the difference between SA and TS is small, both in terms of $Q_{average}$ and CPU-time. The LPSA and LPTS heuristics have about the same $Q_{average}$ as the SA and TS heuristics but CPU-times are higher, since it becomes harder to find feasible setup patterns in the (limited) set of non-fixed variables.

To summarize, the SA and TS heuristics outperform the heuristics $LPRS_1$ and $LPRS_2$ on average, both in terms of (relative) quality of the solutions ($Q_{average}$) and in computation time. A comparison between SA and TS on one hand, and LPSA and LPTS on the other hand, shows that the combined heuristics with respect to $Q_{average}$ perform a little better for low capacitated problems but require much more computation time, since LP_{EFLP} must be solved at initialization. For high capacitated problems it is better to use the SA or TS heuristic, since the required CPU-time is lower. A comparison of the single and multi-pass heuristics shows that the performance of the multi-pass heuristic with respect to $Q_{average}$ is rather good for "simple" product structures. However, as complexity of the product structure increases, the multi-pass heuristic does not seem to perform much better than the single pass heuristic.

Comparing the performance of the SA and TS heuristics a tentative conclusion can be drawn that solutions from SA heuristics are slightly better than solutions from TS heuristics (and the standard deviation is usually smaller) if they run for about the same computation time. However, as reported by Hertz and de Werra [61,109], for other problems and for other parameter settings different conclusions may be obtained.

7.4 Summary and discussion

In this chapter a comparison of (combinations of) LP-based heuristics with tabu search and simulated annealing heuristics for solving the Multilevel Capacitated Lotsizing Problem (MLCLP) is presented. From the computational results it is concluded that simulated annealing and tabu search heuristics perform reasonably well compared to LP-based (rounding) heuristics, both with respect to quality of the solutions and with respect to computational effort required.

Although MLCLP is a very hard problem, it appears that statistical search algorithms like simulated annealing and tabu search provide a promising tool for achieving reasonably good quality solutions. An additional advantage of these methods is that they generate many feasible solutions, (production plans), which can easily be tested for the existence of additional properties, not explicitly taken into account in the model formulation. The main disadvantages of the presented statistical search techniques are, first, that they do not provide the user which direct information about the quality of the solutions (unlike e.g. LP based heuristics, which provide a lower bound as well) and, second, statistical search methods contain a number of parameters, which can only be set by trial and error procedures.

Appendix

Theorem 7.1 (Zero-Inventory Property) *If echelon holding costs are non-negative, there exists an optimal solution to MLCLP, in which at the* uncapacitated levels *production for item i in period t only takes place when inventory is zero at the end of period $t-1$, that is:*

$$I_{i,t-1} x_{i,t} = 0 \text{ for } i \notin \mathcal{C}$$

Proof: Let (x, I) be an optimal solution to MLCLP and suppose that $I_{i,t-1} x_{i,t} > 0$ for some item $i \notin \mathcal{C}$. (Note that $t > 1$ because $I_{i,0} = 0$.) Furthermore, let $q_{i,\tau}$ be the production for item i in period $\tau (= 1, .., t-1)$ for inventory at the end of period $t-1$. Now it is clear that the production of the quantity $I_{i,t-1}$ can be delayed to period t, without violating any of the capacity constraints and without backlogging. Such a delay does not increase the number of setups for item i, since production in period t already takes place. Therefore, setup costs do not increase under this delay.

With respect to the inventory note that inventory for item i in period τ decreases by an amount $q_{i,\tau}$, resulting in cost savings of $h_i \sum_{\tau=1}^{t-1}(t-\tau)q_{i,\tau}$. On the other hand, inventory for item j increases in period τ by an amount $g_{j,i}q_{i,\tau}$, leading to an extra inventory holding cost of $h_j g_{j,i} \sum_{\tau=1}^{t-1}(t-\tau)q_{i,\tau}$.

Thus, in delaying production for item i, the net change in inventory holding costs is equal to:

$$h_i \sum_{\tau=1}^{t-1}(t-\tau)q_{i,\tau} - \sum_{j=1}^{N} h_j g_{j,i} \sum_{\tau=1}^{t-1}(t-\tau)q_{i,\tau}$$

Rewriting this expression in terms of the echelon holding costs for item i ($\tilde{h}_i$), results in a total change in costs of:

$$\tilde{h}_i \sum_{\tau=1}^{t-1}(t-\tau)q_{i,\tau}$$

which is clearly non-negative, since echelon holding costs are assumed to be non-negative.

Therefore, delaying production in the way described above will not result in a cost increase, and consequently, by iteratively delaying production, a production schedule results which satisfies the assertion of Theorem 7.1.

□

Epilogue

In this dissertation we investigate deterministic lotsizing problems. After a discussion of a number of commonly used concepts for production planning (Chapter 1), we apply these concepts to the lotsizing problem. We conclude that, although most of these concepts include procedures to support the production planner in solving the lotsizing problem, it is remarkable that complicating, but often occurring problem components (like capacity restrictions, setup times and sequencing aspects) are ignored to a large extent. In practice, these omissions may cause serious problems, often leading to infeasible and unworkable production schedules. To support the production planner in determining more accurate production schedules, Management Scientists started research on mathematical models dealing with the above-mentioned problems already early in this century.

Our contribution to this line of research is twofold. *First*, we provide the reader with an extensive overview of the *"current state-of-the-art"* in lotsizing, and *second*, we introduce some new model formulations and solution procedures, in which capacity restrictions, setup times and sequencing aspects are considered explicitly.

In Part I of this thesis we evaluate previous research on the single-level lotsizing problem. We compare in Chapter 2 a number of commonly used model formulations, both from a theoretical point of view (computational complexity), and from a practical point of view (underlying assumptions and algorithms). In the remainder of Part I we focus on a recently introduced formulation for the lotsizing problem, called the Discrete Lotsizing and Scheduling Problem (DLSP).

In Chapter 3 we introduce a notation to denote various problem extensions of DLSP, including problems with non-zero setup times, parallel machine problems, and problems with sequence-dependent setup costs. In the sequel of this chapter we derive computational complexity results for problems covered by our problem notation. The main results are: *(i) the NP-Hardness of the multi-item, single machine optimization problem, (ii) the NP-Completeness of the feasibility problem for the multi-item DLSP in presence of setup times, (iii) the NP-Completeness of the feasibility problem for the general parallel machine DLSP*, and *(iv) the existence of a polynomial time algorithm for the parallel identical machine problem with zero setup costs and zero setup times.*

These complexity results correspond to complexity results obtained for alternative model formulations of the multi-item capacitated lotsizing problem, such as the Economic Lotsizing and Scheduling Problem (ELSP), the Capacitated Lotsizing Problem (CLSP), and the Continuous Setup Lotsizing Problem (CSLP). Consequently, we conclude that, from a *theoretical* point of view, the multi-item DLSP does not provide advantages over alternative model formulations.

However, in Chapter 4, we demonstrate that the single item, single machine DLSP can be solved in polynomial time, by Dynamic Programming (DP). The same holds true for a non-trivial extension of the problem, in which both setup costs and setup times are considered. Consequently, DLSP is the *only* discrete-time capacitated lotsizing problem considered so far, for which the single item version is solvable in polynomial time.

Moreover, we show that, under several restrictions with respect to the input parameters, the single item, single machine problem can be solved by two alternative *special purpose* procedures. The first procedure is based on solving a reformulation of the original integer program formulation of DLSP. This reformulation shows close resemblance to the formulation of the assignment problem, in that *both* production and setup variables have been substituted by assignment type of variables. We prove that solving the LP-relaxation of this reformulated DLSP naturally leads to optimal all-integer solutions to the original DLSP.

Our second procedure for solving the single item DLSP is based on a DP-algorithm, with a running time of $\mathcal{O}(T \log T)$. It is remarkable that this algorithm is in fact an adaptation of a recently developed algorithm for solving the *uncapacitated* Wagner-Whitin problem.

Finally, we present a set of *valid inequalities*, which can be added to the LP-relaxation of the original integer programming formulation of DLSP, to obtain stronger lower bounds. An interesting topic for future research lies in finding additional sets of valid inequalities, such that a complete description of the convex (integer) hull of the single item DLSP can be obtained. Results of this type would allow the design of successful cutting-plane algorithms for solving various DLSP problems.

From the results obtained in Chapter 4 we conclude that DLSP is the only *capacitated* lotsizing problem for which the single item single machine version is solvable in polynomial time, even in case of non-zero setup times. This result suggests that decomposition algorithms, in which the multi-item problem is decomposed into a number of single item subproblems, may be successful. The empirical study with decomposition algorithms for various multi-item DLSP's, as presented in Chapter 5, confirms this. Especially the Lagrangean relaxation heuristic in [40] for solving the multi-item problem with zero setup times, and the column generation heuristics for the same problem in presence of setup-times, may be considered as some of the few successful attempts in solving larger sized capacitated lotsizing problems to (near) optimality. Interesting future research topics with respect to solution procedures for multi-item problems lie in finding good heuristics for problems with sequence dependent setup costs and/or setup times occur. One way to attack this type of problems may be a search for multi-item valid inequalities, which can be used to improve the decomposition like algorithms for this problem, as suggested in [40].

In Part II of the thesis we consider the multilevel lotsizing problem. An extensive literature overview for the uncapacitated problem (MLLP) is given in Chapter 6. In addition, we present a simple heuristic for MLLP, which relies upon Lagrangean relaxation, Dynamic Programming, and subgradient optimization. From computational experiments it appears that the performance of our heuristic is satisfactory, when independent demand occurs for end-items only, and when production costs are time-independent. This is mainly caused by the fact that in this case a set of non-trivial inequalities can be added to the mixed integer formulation of MLLP, based on a special structure of the optimal solution to MLLP. However, when independent demand occurs for components too, or when production costs become time-dependent, this special structure is lost, and the quality of the heuristic solutions decreases dramatically.

Therefore, an interesting topic for future research is to develop more successful procedures for this general type of MLLP.

The multilevel capacitated lotsizing problem (MLCLP) is considered in Chapter 7. We propose three heuristics for solving a special version of the problem, in which the capacity restriction applies only to a single level in the product structure. The heuristics are based on *(i) rounding-off solutions obtained from a strong LP-formulation for assembly problems, (ii) simulated annealing procedures*, and *(iii) tabu search heuristics*. A computational comparison shows that the statistical search procedures *(ii)* and *(iii)* perform reasonably well, compared to the linear programming based round-off heuristics *(i)*. However, a disadvantage of statistical search heuristics is that they do not provide the user with direct information on the quality of the solutions (lower bounds), and that they contain a number of parameters, which can only be determined by trial and error procedures. Therefore, it may be better to use problem specific algorithms than general purpose statistical search techniques for solving this type of combinatorial optimization problems. Unfortunately, no reasonable alternative procedures are known for solving MLCLP, and therefore a lot of research remain to be done in this area. A first idea which may provide more satisfactory solutions to the multilevel capacitated lotsizing problem is, to consider alternative formulations for it, such as extensions of the single level DLSP to the multilevel problem.

Bibliography

[1] E.H.L. AARTS AND P.J.M. VAN LAARHOVEN. Statistical cooling: a general approach to combinatorial optimization problems. *Philips Journal of Research*, 40(4):193–226, 1985.

[2] P. AFENTAKIS AND B. GAVISH. Optimal lot sizing for complex product structures. *Operations Research*, 34(2):237–249, 1986.

[3] P. AFENTAKIS, B. GAVISH, AND U. KARMARKAR. Computationally efficient optimal solutions to the lotsizing problem in multistage assembly systems. *Management Science*, 30(2):222–239, 1984.

[4] A. AGGARWAL AND J.K. PARK. *Applications of Array Searching to Economic Lot Size Problems.* Technical Report, Massachusetts Institute of Technology, 1990.

[5] R.N. ANTHONY. *Planning and Control Systems: A Framework for Analysis.* Harvard University Press, Cambridge, Mass., 1965.

[6] E. ARKIN, D. JONEJA, AND R. ROUNDY. Computational complexity of uncapacitated multi-echelon production planning problems. *Operations Research Letters*, 8:61–66, 1989.

[7] S. AXSÄTER. *An extension of the Extended Basic Period Approach for Economic Lot Scheduling Problems.* Technical Report, Department of Production Economics, Linköping Institute of Technology, Sweden, 1983.

[8] H.C. BAHL, L.P. RITZMAN, AND J.N.D. GUPTA. Determining lot sizes and resource requirements: a review. *Operations Research*, 35(3):329–345, 1987.

[9] K.R. BAKER. *Lot-sizing procedures and a standard data set: a reconciliation of the literature.* Technical Report NH 03755-1798, The Amos Tuck School of Business Administration, Dartmouth College, Hanover, 1990.

[10] K.R. BAKER, P. DIXON, M.J. MAGAZINE, AND E.A. SILVER. An algorithm for the Dynamic Lot-size Problem with time-varying production capacity constraints. *Management Science*, 24(16):710–720, 1978.

[11] I. BARANY, T.J. VAN ROY, AND L.A. WOLSEY. Strong formulations for multi-item capacitated lotsizing. *Management Science*, 30(10):1255–1261, 1984.

[12] W.L. BERRY. Lot sizing procedures for requirements planning systems: a framework for analysis. *Production and Inventory Management*, 13(2):19–34, 1972.

[13] J.W.M. BERTRAND AND J. WIJNGAARD. The structuring of production control systems. *Operations & Production Management*, 6(2):5–20, 1986.

[14] P.J. BILLINGTON, J. BLACKBURN, J. MAES, R. MILLEN, AND L.N. VAN WASSENHOVE. *Multi-Product Scheduling in Capacitated Multi-Stage Serial Systems.* Technical Report 8908/A, Econometric Institute, Erasmus Universiteit Rotterdam, The Netherlands, 1989.

[15] P.J. BILLINGTON, J.O. McCLAIN, AND L.J. THOMAS. Heuristics for multilevel lot-sizing with a bottleneck. *Management Science*, 32(8):989–1006, 1986.

[16] P.J. BILLINGTON, J.O. McCLAIN, AND L.J. THOMAS. Mathematical programming approaches to capacity-constrained MRP systems: review, formulation and problem reduction. *Management Science*, 29(10):1126–1141, 1983.

[17] G.B. BITRAN AND H.H. YANASSE. Computational complexity of the Capacitated Lot Size Problem. _Management Science_, 28(10):1174–1185, 1982.

[18] J.D. BLACKBURN AND R.A. MILLEN. Improved heuristics for multistage requirements planning systems. _Management Science_, 28(1):44–56, 1982.

[19] E. BOMBERGER. A dynamic programming approach to a lot size scheduling problem. _Management Science_, 12(11):778–784, 1966.

[20] J. BRUNO AND P. DOWNEY. Complexity of task sequencing with deadlines, set-up times and changeover costs. _SIAM J. Comput._, 7(4):393–404, 1978.

[21] G. BUXEY. Production scheduling: practice and theory. _European Journal of Operational Research_, 39(1):17–31, 1989.

[22] J.J. CARRENO. Economic lot scheduling for multiple products on parallel identical processors. _Management Science_, 36(3):348–358, 1990.

[23] D. CATTRYSSE, J. MAES, AND L.N. VAN WASSENHOVE. Set partitioning and column generation heuristics for capacitated dynamic lotsizing. _European Journal of Operational Research_, 46(1):38–47, 1990.

[24] D. CATTRYSSE, M. SALOMON, R. KUIK, AND L.N. VAN WASSENHOVE. _Heuristics for the Discrete Lotsizing and Scheduling Problem with setup times._ Management Report Series 62, Rotterdam School of Management, The Netherlands, 1990. (_Submitted to Management Science_).

[25] W.H. CHEN AND J.M. THIZY. _Analysis of relaxations for the Multi-item Capacitated Lotsizing Problem._ Technical Report 86-103, School of Management & Department of Industrial Engineering, State University at Buffalo, N.Y., 1987.

[26] W.B. CROWSTON AND M.H. WAGNER. Dynamic lot size models for multi-stage assembly systems. *Management Science*, 20(1):14–21, 1973.

[27] J.J. DE MATTEIS AND A.G. MENDOZE. An economic lot sizing technique. *IBM System Journal*, 7:30–46, 1968.

[28] C.M. DELPORTE AND L.J. THOMAS. Lot size and sequencing for *n* products on one facility. *Management Science*, 23(10):1070–1079, 1977.

[29] M. DIABY. *Large-scale capacitated lotsizing by Lagrangean relaxation*. Technical Report 87-38, Faculté des Sciences de l'Administration, Université Laval, Québec, Canada, 1987.

[30] P.S. DIXON AND E.A. SILVER. A heuristic solution procedure for the Multi- Item, Single Level, Limited Capacity, Lotsizing Problem. *Journal of Operations Management*, 2(1):23– 39, 1981.

[31] G. DOBSON. *The Cyclic Lot Scheduling Problem with sequence dependent setups*. Technical Report QM 88-16, The Center for Manufacturing and Operations Management, University of Rochester, 1989.

[32] G. DOBSON. The Economic Lot-Scheduling Problem: achieving feasibility using time-varying lot sizes. *Operations Research*, 15(5):764–771, 1987.

[33] A. DOGRAMACI, J.C. PANAYIOTOPOULOS, AND N.R. ADAM. The Dynamic Lotsizing Problem for multiple items under limited capacity. *AIIE Transactions*, 13(4):294–303, 1981.

[34] C.L. DOLL AND D.C. WHYBARK. An iterative procedure for the Single-Machine Multi-Product Lot Scheduling Problem. *Management Science*, 20(1):50–55, 1973.

[35] P.S. EISENHUT. A dynamic lotsizing algorithm with capacity constraints. *AIIE Transactions*, 7(2):170–176, 1975.

[36] S. ELMAGHRABY. The Economic Lot Scheduling Problem (ELSP): review and extensions. *Management Science*, 24(6):587–598, 1978.

[37] G.D. EPPEN, F.J. GOULD, AND B.P. PASHIGIAN. Extensions of the planning horizon theorem in the dynamic lot size model. *Management Science*, 15(5):268–277, 1969.

[38] G.D. EPPEN AND R.K. MARTIN. Solving multi-item capacitated lot-sizing problems using variable redefinition. *Operations Research*, 35(6):268–277, 1987.

[39] M.L. FISHER. The Lagrangian relaxation method for solving integer programming problems. *Management Science*, 27(1):1–18, 1981.

[40] B. FLEISCHMANN. The Discrete Lot-Sizing and Scheduling Problem. *European Journal of Operational Research*, 44(3):337–348, 1990. *(Appeared in 1988 as technical report.)*.

[41] B. FLEISCHMANN AND T. POPP. *Das dynamische Losgrössenproblem mit reihenfolgeabhängigen Rüstkosten*. Technical Report, Institut für Unternehmensforschung, Universität Hamburg, Germany, 1988.

[42] M. FLORIAN, J.K. LENSTRA, AND A.H.G. RINNOOY KAN. Deterministic production planning: algorithms and complexity. *Management Science*, 26:12–20, 1980.

[43] S. FUJITA. The application of marginal analysis to the Economic Lot Scheduling Problem. *AIIE Transactions*, 10:354–361, 1978.

[44] M.R. GAREY AND D.S. JOHNSON. *Computers and Intractability, A Guide to the Theory of NP-Completeness*. W.H. Freemann and Company, New York, 1979.

[45] R.S. GARFINKEL AND G.L. NEMHAUSER. Set Partitioning Problem: set covering with equality constraints. *Operations Research*, 17:848–856, 1969.

[46] B. GAVISH AND R.E. JOHNSON. A fully polynomial absolute approximation scheme for single product scheduling in a finite capacity facility. *Operations Research*, 38:70–83, 1990.

[47] L.F. GELDERS AND L.N. VAN WASSENHOVE. Production planning: a review. *European Journal of Operational Research*, 7:101–110, 1981.

[48] F. GLOVER. *Tabu Search*. Technical Report 88-3, Center for Applied Artificial Intelligence, Graduate School of Business, University of Colorado, Boulder, 1988.

[49] F. GLOVER AND H.J. GREENBERG. New approaches for heuristic search: a bilateral linkage with artificial intelligence. *European Journal of Operational Research*, 39:119–126, 1989.

[50] T.C. GONDRAN AND M. MINOUX. *Graphs and Algorithms*. John Wiley & Sons, New York, 1975.

[51] T. GORHAM. Dynamic order quantities. *Production and Inventory Management*, 20(1):75–79, 1968.

[52] S.K. GOYAL. Scheduling a multi-product single-machine system. *Operational Research Quarterly*, 24(2):261–266, 1973.

[53] M. GUIGNARD AND M.B. ROSENWEIN. An application-oriented guide for designing Lagrangean dual ascent algorithms. *European Journal of Operational Research*, 43(2):197–205, 1989.

[54] H.O. GÜNTHER. The design of a hierarchical model for production planning and scheduling. In S. Axsäter, Ch. Schneeweiss, and E. Silver, editors, *Lecture Notes in Economics and Mathematical Systems, Volume 266*, pages 227–260, Springer Verlag, Heidelberg, Germany, 1986.

[55] S.T. HACKMAN AND R.C. LEACHMAN. General framework for modeling production. *Management Science*, 35(4):478–495, 1989.

[56] F. HANSSMANN. *Operations Research in Production and Inventory*. John Wiley & Sons, New York, 1962.

[57] F.W. HARRIS. How many parts to make at once. *Factory, The Magazine of Management,* 10(2):135–136, 1913.

[58] A.C. HAX AND D. CANDEA. *Production and Inventory Management.* Printice-Hall Inc., Englewood Cliffs, N.J., 1984.

[59] A.C. HAX AND H.C. MEAL. Hierarchical integration of production planning and scheduling. In M. Geisler, editor, *TIMS Studies in Management Science,* chapter 1, North Holland/American Elsevier, New York, 1975.

[60] T.H.B. HENDRIKS AND J. WESSELS. Repetitive schemes for the single machine, multiproduct lot-size scheduling problem. In *Proceedings of Operations Research Verfahren XXVI,* pages 571–581, 1978.

[61] A. HERTZ AND D. DE WERRA. *The Tabu Search Metaheuristic: How we used it.* Technical Report ORWP 88/13, Département de Mathématiques, École Polytechnique Fédérale de Lausanne, Switserland, 1989.

[62] W. HSU. On the general feasibility test of scheduling lot sizes for several products on one machine. *Management Science,* 29(1):93–105, 1983.

[63] N. KARMARKAR. A new polynomial time algorithm for Linear Programming. *Combinatorica,* 4, 1984.

[64] U.S. KARMARKAR, S. KEKRE, AND S. KEKRE. The Deterministic Lotsizing Problem with startup and reservation costs. *Operations Research,* 35(3):389–398, 1987.

[65] U.S. KARMARKAR AND L. SCHRAGE. The Deterministic Dynamic Product Cycling Problem. *Operations Research,* 33(2):326–345, 1985.

[66] R. KARNI AND Y. ROLL. A heuristic algorithm for the Multiitem Lotsizing Problem with capacity constraints. *AIIE Transactions,* 14(4):249–256, 1982.

[67] L.G. KHACHIAN. A polynomial algorithm for Linear Programming. *Dokl. Akad. Nauk SSSR*, 244:1093–1096, 1979. English translation in Soviet Math. Dokl. 20:191-194,1979.

[68] O. KIRCA. *A heuristic procedure for the Dynamic Lot-Size Problem with set-up time*. Technical Report, Middle East Technical University, Ankara, Turkey, 1990.

[69] R. KUIK AND M. SALOMON. Multilevel Lotsizing Problem: evaluation of a simulated-annealing heuristic. *European Journal of Operational Research*, 45(1):25–37, 1990.

[70] R. KUIK, M. SALOMON, S. VAN HOESEL, AND L.N. VAN WASSENHOVE. *The Single-Item Discrete Lotsizing and Scheduling Problem: Linear Description and Optimization*. Management Report Series 53, Rotterdam School of Management, The Netherlands, 1989. *Submitted to Discrete Applied Mathematics.*

[71] P.J.M. VAN LAARHOVEN AND E.H.L. AARTS. *Simulated Annealing: Theory and Applications*. D. Reidel Publishing Company, Dordrecht, The Netherlands, 1987.

[72] M. LAMBRECHT AND H. VANDERVEKEN. Heuristic procedures for the Single Operation Multi Item Loading Problem. *AIIE Transactions*, 11(4):319–326, 1979.

[73] L.S. LASDON. *Optimization Theory for Large Systems*. The Macmillan Company, Collier MacMillen Lim., London, U.K., 1970.

[74] L.S. LASDON AND R.C. TERJUNG. An efficient algorithm for multi-item scheduling. *Operations Research*, 19:946–969, 1971.

[75] J.M.Y. LEUNG, T.L. MAGNANTI, AND R. VACHANI. Facets and algorithms for capacitated lotsizing. *Mathematical Programming*, 45:331–359, 1989.

[76] S. LOVE. A facilities in series model with nested schedules. *Management Science*, 18:327–338, 1972.

[77] S. LOZANO. *Multilevel Lot-Sizing with a Bottleneck Work Center.* Master's thesis, Katholieke Universiteit Leuven, Belgium, 1989.

[78] J.C. MADIGAN. Scheduling a multi-product single-machine system for an infinite planning period. *Management Science*, 14(11):713–719, 1968.

[79] J. MAES. *Capacitated Lotsizing Techniques in Manufacturing Resource Planning.* Ph.D. thesis, Katholieke Universiteit Leuven, Belgium, 1987.

[80] J. MAES, J. MCCLAIN, AND L.N. VAN WASSENHOVE. *Multilevel Capacitated Lotsizing: Complexity and LP-Based Heuristics.* Technical Report, Econometric Institute, Erasmus Universiteit Rotterdam, The Netherlands, 1989. (*To appear in European Journal of Operational Research*).

[81] J. MAES AND L.N. VAN WASSENHOVE. A simple heuristic for the Multi-Item Single Level Capacitated Lot Sizing Problem. *Letters of Operations Research*, 4(6):265–274, 1986.

[82] J. MAES AND L.N. VAN WASSENHOVE. Multi-item single-level capacitated dynamic lot-sizing heuristics: a general review. *Journal of the Operational Research Society*, 39(11):991–1004, 1988.

[83] T.L. MAGNANTI AND R. VACHANI. A strong cutting-plane algorithm for production scheduling with changeover costs. *Operations Research*, 38(3):456–473, 1990.

[84] A.S. MANNE. Programming of economic lot sizes. *Management Science*, 4:115–135, 1958.

[85] R. DE MATTA AND M. GUIGNARD. *Production Scheduling with Sequence-Independent Changeover Cost.* Technical Report, Wharton School, University of Pennsylvania, 1989.

[86] J.O. MCCLAIN, L.J. THOMAS, AND E. N. WEISS. Efficient solutions to a linear programming model for production scheduling

with capacity constraints and no initial stock. *IIE Transactions*, 21(2):144–152, 1989.

[87] J.A.E.E. VAN NUNEN AND J. WESSELS. Multi item lot size determination and scheduling under capacity constraints. *European Journal of Operational Research*, 2(1):36–41, 1978.

[88] J. ORLICKY. *Material Requirements Planning.* McGraw-Hill, New York, 1975.

[89] Y. POCHET. Valid inequalities and separation for capacitated economic lot sizing. *Operations Research Letters*, 7:109–116, 1988.

[90] Y. POCHET AND L.A. WOLSEY. *Solving Multi-Item Lot-Sizing Problems using strong cutting planes.* CORE Discussion Paper 8834, Center for Operations Research and Econometrics, Louvain-la-Neuve, Belgium, 1988.

[91] P. RHODES. A paint industry production planning and smoothing system. *Production and Inventory Management*, 18(4):17–29, 1977.

[92] K. ROSLING. *Optimal Lot-Sizing for Dynamic Assembly Systems.* Technical Report 152, Linköping Institute of Technology, Sweden, 1985.

[93] D.M. RYAN AND J.C. FALKNER. On the integer properties of scheduling set partitioning models. *European Journal of Operational Research*, 35(3):165–177, 1988.

[94] M. SALOMON, L. KROON, R. KUIK, AND L.N. VAN WASSENHOVE. *The Discrete Lotsizing and Scheduling Problem.* Management Report Series 30, Rotterdam School of Management, The Netherlands, 1989.

[95] M. SALOMON, L. KROON, R. KUIK, AND L.N. VAN WASSENHOVE. *Some extensions of the Discrete Lotsizing and Scheduling Problem.* Management Report Series 52, Rotterdam School of

Management, The Netherlands, 1989. (*To appear in Management Science*).

[96] L. SCHRAGE. *User Manual for Linear, Integer and Quadratic Programming with LINDO*. The Scientific Press, Redwood City, 1987.

[97] E.A. SILVER AND H.C. MEAL. A heuristic for selecting lot size quantities for the case of a deterministic time-varying demand rate and discrete opportunities for replenishment. *Production and Inventory Management*, 14(2):64–74, 1973.

[98] E.A. SILVER AND R. PETERSON. *Decision Systems for Inventory Management and Production Planning*. John Wiley & Sons, New York, 1985.

[99] M.F. STANGARD AND S.K. GUPTA. A note on Bomberger's approach to lot size scheduling: heuristic proposed. *Management Science*, 15(7):449–452, 1969.

[100] J.M. THIZY AND L.N. VAN WASSENHOVE. Lagrangian relaxation for the Multi-Item Capacitated Lotsizing Problem: a heuristic implementation. *IIE Transactions*, 17(4):308–313, 1985.

[101] W.W. TRIGEIRO, L.J. THOMAS, AND J.O. MCCLAIN. Capacitated lot sizing with setup times. *Management Science*, 35(3):353–366, 1989.

[102] L.N. VAN WASSENHOVE AND M.A. DE BODT. Capacitated lot sizing for injection molding: a case study. *Journal of the Operational Research Society*, 34(6):489–501, 1983.

[103] L.N. VAN WASSENHOVE AND P. VANDERHENST. Planning production in a bottleneck department. *European Journal of Operational Research*, 12:127–137, 1983.

[104] A.F. VEINOTT. Minimum concave-cost solution of Leontief substitution models of multi-facility inventory systems. *Operations Research*, 17(2):262–291, 1969.

[105] A.F. VEINOTT. Unpublished class notes for the Program in Operations Research at Stanford University. 1963.

[106] A.P.M. WAGELMANS, C.P.M. VAN HOESEL, AND A.W.J. KOLEN. *Economic Lot-Sizing: An $\mathcal{O}(N \log N)$ algorithm that runs in linear time in the Wagner-Whitin case.* Technical Report 8952/A, Econometric Institute, Erasmus Universiteit Rotterdam, The Netherlands, 1989.

[107] H.W. WAGNER AND T.H. WHITIN. Dynamic version of the economic lot size model. *Management Science*, 5(1):88–96, 1958.

[108] H.W. WAGNER AND T.H. WHITIN. A postscript to 'dynamic problems' in the theory of the firm. *Naval Research Logistics Quarterly*, 7(1):7–12, 1960.

[109] D. DE WERRA AND A. HERTZ. Tabu search techniques: a tutorial and an application to neural networks. *OR Spektrum*, 11:131–141, 1989.

[110] E. ZABEL. Some generalizations of an inventory planning horizon theorem. *Management Science*, 10(3):465–471, 1964.

[111] W. ZANGWILL. A backlogging model and a multiechelon model of a dynamic economic lot size production system. *Management Science*, 15(9):506–527, 1969.

[112] W. ZANGWILL. A deterministic multiproduct, multifacility production and inventory model. *Operations Research*, 14(3):486–507, 1966.

Vol. 318: T. Doup, Simplicial Algorithms on the Simplotope. VIII, 262 pages. 1988.

Vol. 319: D.T. Luc, Theory of Vector Optimization. VIII, 173 pages. 1989.

Vol. 320: D. van der Wijst, Financial Structure in Small Business. VII, 181 pages. 1989.

Vol. 321: M. Di Matteo, R.M. Goodwin, A. Vercelli (Eds.), Technological and Social Factors in Long Term Fluctuations. Proceedings. IX, 442 pages. 1989.

Vol. 322: T. Kollintzas (Ed.), The Rational Expectations Equilibrium Inventory Model. XI, 269 pages. 1989.

Vol. 323: M.B.M. de Koster, Capacity Oriented Analysis and Design of Production Systems. XII, 245 pages. 1989.

Vol. 324: I.M. Bomze, B.M. Pötscher, Game Theoretical Foundations of Evolutionary Stability. VI, 145 pages. 1989.

Vol. 325: P. Ferri, E. Greenberg, The Labor Market and Business Cycle Theories. X, 183 pages. 1989.

Vol. 326: Ch. Sauer, Alternative Theories of Output, Unemployment, and Inflation in Germany: 1960–1985. XIII, 206 pages. 1989.

Vol. 327: M. Tawada, Production Structure and International Trade. V, 132 pages. 1989.

Vol. 328: W. Güth, B. Kalkofen, Unique Solutions for Strategic Games. VII, 200 pages. 1989.

Vol. 329: G. Tillmann, Equity, Incentives, and Taxation. VI, 132 pages. 1989.

Vol. 330: P.M. Kort, Optimal Dynamic Investment Policies of a Value Maximizing Firm. VII, 185 pages. 1989.

Vol. 331: A. Lewandowski, A.P. Wierzbicki (Eds.), Aspiration Based Decision Support Systems. X, 400 pages. 1989.

Vol. 332: T.R. Gulledge, Jr., L.A. Litteral (Eds.), Cost Analysis Applications of Economics and Operations Research. Proceedings. VII, 422 pages. 1989.

Vol. 333: N. Dellaert, Production to Order. VII, 158 pages. 1989.

Vol. 334: H.-W. Lorenz, Nonlinear Dynamical Economics and Chaotic Motion. XI, 248 pages. 1989.

Vol. 335: A.G. Lockett, G. Islei (Eds.), Improving Decision Making in Organisations. Proceedings. IX, 606 pages. 1989.

Vol. 336: T. Puu, Nonlinear Economic Dynamics. VII, 119 pages. 1989.

Vol. 337: A. Lewandowski, I. Stanchev (Eds.), Methodology and Software for Interactive Decision Support. VIII, 309 pages. 1989.

Vol. 338: J.K. Ho, R.P. Sundarraj, DECOMP: an Implementation of Dantzig-Wolfe Decomposition for Linear Programming. VI, 206 pages. 1989.

Vol. 339: J. Terceiro Lomba, Estimation of Dynamic Econometric Models with Errors in Variables. VIII, 116 pages. 1990.

Vol. 340: T. Vasko, R. Ayres, L. Fontvieille (Eds.), Life Cycles and Long Waves. XIV, 293 pages. 1990.

Vol. 341: G.R. Uhlich, Descriptive Theories of Bargaining. IX, 165 pages. 1990.

Vol. 342: K. Okuguchi, F. Szidarovszky, The Theory of Oligopoly with Multi-Product Firms. V, 167 pages. 1990.

Vol. 343: C. Chiarella, The Elements of a Nonlinear Theory of Economic Dynamics. IX, 149 pages. 1990.

Vol. 344: K. Neumann, Stochastic Project Networks. XI, 237 pages. 1990.

Vol. 345: A. Cambini, E. Castagnoli, L. Martein, P. Mazzoleni, S. Schaible (Eds.), Generalized Convexity and Fractional Programming with Economic Applications. Proceedings, 1988. VII, 361 pages. 1990.

Vol. 346: R. von Randow (Ed.), Integer Programming and Related Areas. A Classified Bibliography 1984–1987. XIII, 514 pages. 1990.

Vol. 347: D. Ríos Insua, Sensitivity Analysis in Multi-objective Decision Making. XI, 193 pages. 1990.

Vol. 348: H. Störmer, Binary Functions and their Applications. VIII, 151 pages. 1990.

Vol. 349: G.A. Pfann, Dynamic Modelling of Stochastic Demand for Manufacturing Employment. VI, 158 pages. 1990.

Vol. 350: W.-B. Zhang, Economic Dynamics. X, 232 pages. 1990.

Vol. 351: A. Lewandowski, V. Volkovich (Eds.), Multiobjective Problems of Mathematical Programming. Proceedings, 1988. VII, 315 pages. 1991.

Vol. 352: O. van Hilten, Optimal Firm Behaviour in the Context of Technological Progress and a Business Cycle. XII, 229 pages. 1991.

Vol. 353: G. Ricci (Ed.), Decision Processes in Economics. Proceedings, 1989. III, 209 pages. 1991.

Vol. 354: M. Ivaldi, A Structural Analysis of Expectation Formation. XII, 230 pages. 1991.

Vol. 355: M. Salomon, Deterministic Lotsizing Models for Production Planning. VII, 158 pages. 1991.